SUSTAINABLE VENTURING

ENTREPRENEURIAL OPPORTUNITY IN THE TRANSITION TO A SUSTAINABLE ECONOMY

Thomas J. Dean

Department of Management,
Colorado State University

WITH CONTRIBUTIONS BY JACOB T. CASTILLO

D0145092

PEARSON

Boston Columbus Indianapolis New York San Francisco Upper Saddle River
Amsterdam Cape Town Dubai London Madrid Milan Munich Paris Montréal Toronto
Delhi Mexico City São Paulo Sydney Hong Kong Seoul Singapore Taipei Tokyo

Editor in Chief: *Stephanie Wall*
Acquisitions Editor: *Sarah Parker McCabe*
Director of Editorial Services: *Ashley Santora*
Managing Editor: *Judy Leale*
Editorial Project Manager: *Claudia Fernandes*
Editorial Assistant: *Ashlee Bradbury*
Director of Marketing: *Maggie Moylan*
Senior Marketing Manager: *Erin Gardner*
Marketing Assistant: *Gianni Sandri*
Production Project Manager: *Meghan DeMaio*
Creative Art Director: *Jayne Conte*
Cover Designer: *Karen Salzbach*
Full-Service Project Management: *Munesh Kumar*
Composition: *iEnergizer Aptara®, Inc.*
Printer/Binder/Cover Printer: *Courier Companies*
Text Font: *10/12 Times Ten LT Std*

Credits and acknowledgments borrowed from other sources and reproduced, with permission, in this textbook appear on the appropriate page within text.

Library of Congress Cataloging-in-Publication Data

Dean, Thomas J.,
  Sustainable venturing : entrepreneurial opportunity in the transition to a sustainable economyb/ Thomas J. Dean, Department of Management, Colorado State University; written with the assistance of Jacob T. Castillo.
    pages cm
  ISBN-13: 978-0-13-604489-5
  ISBN-10: 0-13-604489-1
  1. Social entrepreneurship. 2. Entrepreneurship—Environmental aspects. 3. Technological innovations–Environmental aspects. 4. Social responsibility of business. I. Castillo, Jacob T. II. Title.
  HD60.D347 2014
  658.1'1—dc23

2013000194

10 9 8 7 6 5 4 3 2 1

ISBN 10: 0-13-604489-1
ISBN 13: 978-0-13-604489-5

Dedication

To my mother, Marie Dean

*"For I dipt into the future far as human eye could see,
Saw the vision of the world and all the wonder that would be."*
—Lord Alfred Tennyson

ALFRED, LORD TENNYSON, 1842. Locksley Hall, verses 6065,
The Poetical Works of Alfred, Lord Tennyson, p. 111

BRIEF CONTENTS

CONTENTS

PREFACE

Sustainable venturing is about harnessing the innovative power of entrepreneurship to solve global, social, and environmental challenges. From innovative new business models to new technical solutions and changing economic systems, opportunities for sustainable venturing abound. Sustainable venturing varies from local small business solutions with an environmental flair to emerging high-growth ventures delivering technologies in alternative energy, clean water, and efficiency. Regardless of their focus or magnitude, sustainable ventures are transforming the nature of business, and they can do so while providing financial return to entrepreneurs, their investors, and their organizations.

The prospect of doing well for the environment and society while operating an economically sustainable venture is exciting to potential entrepreneurs and global citizens alike. Increasingly, it seems students want to accomplish both good for society and good for themselves. This book attempts to show how that might be accomplished, and how entrepreneurship can be used as a transformative mechanism in our economic system.

At its core, this book is about engaging economic incentive systems to drive ecologically and socially sustainable behaviors and outcomes. The underlying philosophy is that the capitalistic system is a powerful means to create value for society, and the entrepreneur is the engine of that value creation. This text views capitalism and entrepreneurship as the solutions to our social and environmental challenges, and sustainable entrepreneurs as active participants in the creation of incentives for more sustainable behaviors.

Sustainable Venturing begins Chapter 1 with an introduction to the meaning and arena of sustainable venturing. Chapters 2 and 3 provide students with a broader understanding of the workings of economic systems and how entrepreneurs can interact with those systems, both capturing and creating opportunities in the dynamics of changing economic institutions. These chapters embrace concepts from the fields of environmental and welfare economics to help explain our global, social, and environmental challenges as well as the strategies entrepreneurs can use to overcome these challenges and create economic opportunity.

Chapter 4 is devoted to the exciting and growing concept of social entrepreneurship, which prioritizes social contribution in the development of new businesses. Chapter 5 turns to the practice of environmental marketing and outlines opportunities for the marketing of products with environmental attributes. It emphasizes the unique ways, sometimes unexpected, that organizations have succeeded by making environmental attributes part of their product and promotional strategies.

Chapters 6 and 7 focus on some of the practical aspects of creating a sustainable venture, covering how to launch and finance ventures with positive social and environmental goals and contributions. Chapter 6 covers six elements of the successful sustainable venture including mission, values, planning, legal form, team, and metrics. Chapter 7 discusses the process of funding and the unique sources of financing available to the sustainable venture.

Sustainable Venturing is designed for use in courses in sustainable, environmental, and social entrepreneurship. It serves as the perfect content companion to courses that integrate case studies, speakers, or experiential exercises to engage students in learning about the opportunities for entrepreneurship in sustainability. The text may also serve broader entrepreneurship courses wherein the instructor wishes to dedicate some portion of the class to social and environmental entrepreneurship. It may also be utilized within environmental science, policy, or management curriculum as an introduction to the business side of sustainability and environmental issues. It is written in a manner that is applicable to both graduate and undergraduate student audiences.

Sustainable Venturing covers a host of concepts, topics, and tools relevant to identifying opportunities and implementing a business with positive social and environmental outcomes. It also delivers examples of business models that have contributed to sustainability across a broad array of sectors. The examples demonstrate the methods used to create and capture value in the process of sustainable venturing. Finally, the book's focus on resolving system failures through entrepreneurial action provides a unique perspective, one that will hopefully lead sustainable entrepreneurs to thoughtful approaches that allow the simultaneous achievement of economic, social, and environmental sustainability.

SUPPLEMENTS

At www.pearsonhighered.com/irc, the following supplements are available to adopting instructors for download. Registration is simple and gives you immediate access to new titles and new editions. If you ever need assistance, our dedicated technical support team is ready to help with the supplements that accompany this text. Visit http://247.pearsoned.com/ for answers to frequently asked questions and toll-free user support phone numbers.

- Instructor's Manual
- PowerPoint Slides

COMPANION WEBSITE

A useful companion website, www.pearsonhighered.com/entrepreneurship, offers free access to teaching resources for all books in the Prentice Hall Entrepreneurship Series including additional activities, links to latest research, sample entrepreneurship curriculum and syllabi, teaching tips, and web resource links.

COURSESMART eTEXTBOOKS

CourseSmart eTextbooks were developed for students looking to save on required or recommended textbooks. Students simply select their eText by title or author and purchase immediate access to the content for the duration of the course using any major credit card. With a CourseSmart eText, students can search for specific keywords or page numbers, take notes online, print out reading assignments that incorporate lecture notes, and bookmark important passages for later review. For more information or to purchase a CourseSmart eTextbook, visit www.coursesmart.com.

ACKNOWLEDGMENTS

As with any significant endeavor, many individuals contributed to this book. I would first like to acknowledge the support and encouragement of Pearson Prentice-Hall's Entrepreneurship Series Editors, Drs. Duane Ireland and Michael Morris, without whose support and encouragement this book would not have been completed. I'm particularly grateful to Jacob Castillo, who wrote the first version of Chapter 6 and contributed editorially and conceptually to many other parts of the manuscript.

I would also like to thank those who contributed to the development of the ideas inherent in this book. In particular, authors in the fields of environmental economics and institutional economics laid the foundation for my intellectual contributions on the linkages between environmental issues and entrepreneurship theory.

The creativity and drive of sustainable entrepreneurs in Colorado and beyond have also been a source of encouragement, motivation, and validation. As they have succeeded in their ventures, I have been reassured that the ideas presented in *Sustainable Venturing* work in practice. I would also like to acknowledge some of those who supported me in the early days of my efforts at the intersection of environmental issues and entrepreneurship: Dale Meyer, David Payne, Alison Peters, and Paul Jerde.

My inspiration comes from my mother, a social entrepreneur whose example of caring, hard work, and seemingly never-ending willingness to serve is unparalleled in my entire life's experience. I credit my equanimity to both my father and my brother, who exemplify the characteristics of generosity, compassion, and integrity. My wife's love is the foundation for my ability to keep moving on the projects I pursue. My sons' laughter reminds me every day to smile and enjoy, and their words and futures encourage me to make a difference in the world.

ABOUT THE AUTHOR

Thomas J. Dean is Professor of Entrepreneurship and Sustainable Enterprise in the Department of Management at Colorado State University. He earned his PhD from the University of Colorado and his MBA from Oklahoma State University. He also received a BS in Environmental Resource Management from The Pennsylvania State University. He currently teaches in Colorado State University's innovative Global, Social, and Sustainable Enterprise MBA program. His previous academic appointments include the University of Colorado, where he served as the Faculty Director of the Deming Center for Entrepreneurship, and the University of Tennessee.

Dr. Dean created the first course in sustainable venturing in 2001 and has since gone on to publish pioneering conceptual work at the intersection of entrepreneurship, environmental issues, and sustainability. He also founded the first dedicated business plan competition for student clean technology ventures and sits on the advisory boards for the School of Global Environmental Sustainability and the Clean Energy Supercluster at Colorado State University. He also engages with student and nonstudent ventures and has worked in an executive capacity at a clean-tech venture. He served as Chair of the Entrepreneurship Division of the Academy of Management and founded one of the first business-school environmental management programs in the United States.

Dr. Dean has published articles on entrepreneurship and environmental issues in journals such as the *Academy of Management Journal,* the *Strategic Management Journal,* the *Journal of Business Venturing,* and the *Journal of Environmental Economics and Management.*

CHAPTER 1

INTRODUCTION TO SUSTAINABLE VENTURING

INTRODUCTION

In 1977, Colorado entrepreneur Steve Demos founded WhiteWave soy foods with the dream of bringing the nutritional and environmental benefits of soy food products to U.S. consumers. Starting with $500 in capital, Demos began making tofu products in his bathtub and walked them to local customers in a red wagon. By the mid-1980s, White Wave was shipping soy products nationally to over 1000 natural food stores, but struggled financially. White Wave was still a small company with limited appeal to larger markets. Soymilk, one of its primary product lines, remained hidden on the dry shelves in unappealing aseptic boxes. That's when Demos decided to combine his passion for soy products with professional marketing and entrepreneurial skills. White Wave reformulated its soymilk and created the Silk brand. The product was eventually placed beside milk in the refrigerated aisle. With the new product, appealing branding, and attractive shelf space, sales grew rapidly and expanded beyond natural food stores to national grocers. Dean Foods, the largest producer of milk in the United States, purchased the company at a valuation of over $200 million. Today, the White Wave Division leads Dean Foods' forays into natural and organic food products, holding brands such as Silk, Horizon Organic, and Land O'Lakes.[1, 2] Demos, meanwhile, continues his entrepreneurial endeavors in natural foods, having recently founded NextFoods. The company's first product, GoodBelly, is a popular probiotic fruit drink that builds digestive health.

After spending his college summers selling books door-to-door, a young Quayle Hodek turned his sights on renewable energy. Founding Renewable

Choice in 2001, Quayle applied his sales abilities to the marketing of renewable energy and hired college students to sell renewable energy credits to residential customers during their summer break. No easy task, but the strategy was successful enough to keep the company going. Then interest and demand from commercial customers and green builders bloomed. Within the span of only a few years, Renewable Choice had helped industry leaders such as Whole Foods, Vail Resorts, and Gander Mountain offset their electric power usage with renewable energy and carbon offsets. The company now employs more than twenty-five people and has been a driving force in the marketing of renewable energy.

Responding to the lack of reliable electrical power infrastructure in Kenya, entrepreneur Simon Mwacharo began experimenting with wind turbines. He enlisted friends with electrical experience to help design charge controllers, generators, fiberglass blades, and towers. He created CraftSkills East Africa Limited, which builds and installs low-cost, locally designed wind turbines. The company markets to rural homes, schools, hotels, health facilities, and shops. They have installed over eighty wind turbines, bringing power, lighting, security, and cell phone charging to customers. In one case, they built a wind turbine and distribution system that provides power to a thirty-hut village in a remote valley of Kenya. To add value, the company connects its devices to water pumps, LED lighting systems, and battery-charging centers.[3, 4]

These entrepreneurs and the companies they created are not just individual stories of success, they portend the next entrepreneurial revolution—that of sustainable venturing. Driven by fundamental trends in our global economy, sustainable entrepreneurs are creating a more ecologically, socially, and economically sustainable way of life. They do so, not so much at the expense of profit, but at the behest of it. For, as resource scarcity, population, and climate change alter the economic fabric of global society, new opportunities for profit are arising. The sustainable entrepreneurs who recognize these changes and create new technologies, products, and business models that enhance the sustainability of our global resources stand to benefit. Entrepreneurs helped create our present, and sustainable entrepreneurs will pioneer our future.

ENTREPRENEURS: OUR MODERN-DAY PIONEERS

Entrepreneurship, *the process of creating value by bringing together a unique combination of resources to develop and pursue an economic opportunity,* is one of the most powerful forces in the world today. From Ford Motor Company, to Apple Computer, to Google, entrepreneurial companies have driven technological development, changed the way we live our lives, and fundamentally altered the course of human history. From food production, health care, and transportation, to modern conveniences and entertainment, entrepreneurs in many industries have created better products and services and delivered them in increasingly efficient ways. Thanks to entrepreneurs and the market systems that drive them, developed societies live today in a world of prosperity and capability only dreamed of by earlier generations.

Entrepreneurs are powerful drivers of positive change because they *tend to be rewarded for creating value for society and its members.* This was the fundamental realization of famed economist Adam Smith when he stated that "by directing that industry in such a manner as its produce may be of greatest value, he intends only his own gain and, he is in this, as in many other cases, led by an invisible hand to promote an end which was no part of his intention. . . . By pursuing his own interest he frequently promotes that of society more effectually than when he really intends to promote it."[5] In other words, when entrepreneurs create value by offering products and services that people want and need, they increase their chances of realizing economic profits while also making society better off.

The potential to achieve profit is commonly referred to as *economic opportunity.* At any given time, opportunities exist within the system of rewards present in the global economy. Opportunities can also be created through changes in the system of rewards over time. Many opportunities are hidden or otherwise difficult to perceive or pursue, but that is what allows their continued existence and creates the potential for profit. The opportunities that are effortlessly observed and easily exploited tend to disappear quickly due to the competitive nature of markets, so they are transient in the sense that they can both disappear quickly and be created as the result of fundamental changes in demand, supply, and other conditions. Such opportunities are windows that open and close according to both the rewards available at any given time and the extent of competition for those rewards.

Opportunities have also been referred to as *market gaps or imperfections,* implying the potential to fulfill new customer demand conditions or existing demands in new ways. As such, economic opportunities are fundamentally linked to the creation of value for customers, or society, more broadly. Opportunities are, in their essence, problems waiting to be solved, holding rewards for those who solve them. The sustainability of our environmental resources is one of the biggest problems, and opportunities, facing society today.

"HOUSTON, WE HAVE A PROBLEM"

In 1968, when lunar astronauts snapped the first photograph of Earth rising from the moon, one thing became immediately clear: We all live on a single planet in an otherwise rather desolate expanse of space.[6] From the ground, Earth appears vast and unending. From space, it appears small, isolated, and precious. The fact is that we have the resources of only one Earth. With the exception of the input of solar energy, our planet is what systems-thinkers call a *closed system:* It has limits, and it is constrained. Earth's resources are scarce, and they are valuable because they provide the means by which we eat, drink, walk, play, laugh, and love.

Ecosystem services are the services that Earth's ecological systems provide to human existence. In other words, they represent the value that the ecosystems create for human society. Ecosystem services include a host of benefits provided by the natural environment, including regulation of the air we breathe, the stabilization of our climate, the supply of water, the production of food and raw materials, and recreation. One estimate of the value of these services places their annual value at $33 trillion dollars, greater than the global gross national product.[7] Regardless of whether such numbers are accurate, our economy and civilization are fundamentally reliant on ecosystem services and on our planet's ecological resources.

Yet the *ecological footprint* of our economic activities is arguably greater than the capacity of the ecological systems that provide those services.[8] Current estimates of humanity's ecological footprint, the burden of our activities on the environment, suggest that it would require 1.4 Earths to sustain the current level of economic activity.[9] While climate change seems to present the most ominous challenge, the loss of biodiversity, diminishing freshwater supply, soil erosion, air pollution, infectious disease, and degradation of fisheries remain serious and costly issues. Overuse of natural systems foretells the eventual diminishment of the valuable environmental resources (often referred to as *natural capital*) upon which we rely. The number of people that natural capital can support, and their quality of life, depends on the magnitude of the earth's resources and the way in which we use them. Many argue that the global economy, as currently constructed, is not ecologically sustainable—that is, it does not stand up to the test of *sustainable development,* which is to meet the needs of the present without compromising the ability of future generations to meet their own needs.[10] Embedded in the idea of sustainable development is the realization that any economic activity that is not socially and ecologically sustainable will not be economically sustainable in the long run either. Economic development, social value creation, and environmental preservation are linked at their core.

THE BIGGEST OPPORTUNITY

Sustainable venturing is the process of creating socially and ecologically sustainable value by bringing together a unique combination of resources to pursue an economic opportunity. *Ecologically sustainable value* is value created for society and its members that simultaneously sustains or enhances the social and ecological resources of the planet. Sustainable entrepreneurship can be seen as a subset of the larger concept of entrepreneurship, but as society adapts to the realities of the present and future, the two will become increasingly aligned. In this book, we use the terms *sustainable venturing, sustainable entrepreneurship,* and *environmental entrepreneurship* as similar or equivalent. We also discuss the concept of social entrepreneurship, as we see social issues as an important aspect of sustainable development.

If society is to be successful in the long term, the system of rewards must create a context in which unsustainable entrepreneurship is not economically profitable. More important, as the system of rewards that motivates entrepreneurs evolves through increasing recognition of our global challenges, opportunities for sustainable entrepreneurship will grow substantially. This process of becoming more environmentally aware, and open to new economic opportunities as a result, is already underway.

In 1990, Francis Cairncross of the *Economist* wrote that the environment may turn out to be "the biggest opportunity for enterprise and invention the industrial world has ever seen."[11] Today, Ms. Cairncross's prognostication is manifest in a multitude of industries around the world. Innovative entrepreneurs across the globe have started businesses that are creating rewards for them and for environment. These sustainable entrepreneurs are not easily categorized into a single type, nor do they fit within any single industry. Rather, they come in many shapes and sizes, and span a host of sectors. They do share the common attribute of offering new products, services, or business models that increase our social and ecological sustainability.

Most celebrated and exciting of these sustainable ventures are the technology start-ups with high growth potential, most commonly referred to as clean-tech (or green-tech) ventures. Some clean-tech ventures hold the prospect of fundamentally changing the delivery of products and services and have been a magnet for recent investors. Tesla Motors in California offers a completely electric car that can accelerate from 0 to 60 miles per hour in 3.9 seconds while generating one-tenth of the pollution of comparable sports cars. Numerous companies are developing advanced lithium batteries with higher power and longer life, potentially enabling the production of lower-cost electric vehicles while also reducing waste and materials use. Clipper Windpower developed a wind turbine technology that reduces loading on its internal mechanism, thereby increasing reliability. The result is lower turbine operating costs and more competitive prices for wind-generated electricity. Clean-energy ventures have garnered the largest share of clean-tech investments, but start-ups in other sectors have been robust as well. The clean-tech revolution comprises companies in energy efficiency, energy storage, water purification and management, advanced materials, recycling, agriculture, and manufacturing.

But sustainable entrepreneurs don't just include high-growth technology ventures. A host of others are founding small businesses and lifestyle companies that provide a living while allowing them to pursue their passions. Nate Burger, the Eco-Handyman, provides a variety of household services with a green flair. Recent trends toward energy-efficient and nontoxic renovations have allowed him to build a healthy contracting business. Entrepreneur and innovative manager Blake Jones founded Namaste Solar after spending years installing remote solar systems in Nepal. Namaste Solar has become renown for its collaborative, equitable, and fun company culture, as well as a leading installer of solar energy systems in homes and commercial buildings.

Other sustainable ventures aren't driven by complex technology but have become significant and notable businesses. Horizon Organic grew quickly after introducing its line of organic dairy products with the attractive "happy cow" icon. Horizon is now the leading brand of organic milk in the United States and helped convert hundreds of thousands of acres to organic farming. Evolution Markets, an emissions-allowance trading firm, employs over eighty energy and emissions brokers worldwide, has built a reputation as one of the top emissions-trading and financial companies in the world, and has experienced substantial growth as a result of global climate change policy. Rocky Mountain Sustainable Enterprises has built a substantial business by recycling used cooking oil into biofuel. Their RecycOil service collects used cooking oil from restaurants, processes the waste into diesel, and offsets the consumption of fossil fuels.[12]

Some sustainable entrepreneurs are of the corporate type. Kevin Beaty and his team at Eaton Company helped develop a transmission system for diesel electric hybrids that is now utilized by FedEx and the United Parcel Service. Starting about five years behind their competition, Eaton Company succeeded by letting customer input drive technology development. Their hybrid systems can reduce fuel consumption in stop-and-go truck applications by as much 60 percent. Toyota's and Honda's hybrid automobile offerings have had similar success, offering substantial increases in fuel economy. But probably the biggest corporate effort into environmental entrepreneurship is that of General Electric (GE). In 2005, GE surprised the world when it announced its ecomagination initiative. Chief Executive Officer Jeff Immelt announced that "green is green" and that producing environmentally friendly and energy-efficient products would drive revenue growth and profitability in their company. The ecomagination initiative launched technological and product development in a multitude of sectors including compact fluorescent bulbs, energy star appliances, locomotive engines, solar modules, and energy-efficient home improvement loans.

In other cases, the products sustainable entrepreneurs create are not as obviously sustainable, but their delivery or production are. New Belgium Brewing brews its high-quality beers at a highly efficient and 100 percent wind-powered facility. The company uses anaerobic digesters to transform its waste stream into energy for the brewery. It also uses 20 percent less water in the brewing process and has one of the most energy-efficient brewing facilities in the world. The company has also developed a values-driven culture of ecological sustainability and community involvement which helps drive innovation and reduce ecological impact. Outdoor apparel manufacturer Patagonia takes a similar approach. "Committed to the Core," the company, is an example of what environmental entrepreneurs can accomplish. From their efforts to preserve important ecosystems to the promotion of organic cotton, Patagonia has been a leader in implementing and promoting more sustainable business practices.

DRIVERS OF OPPORTUNITY: THE SIX C'S

The multitude of opportunities for sustainable venturing is being driven by fundamental trends in our global society and economy. Though these trends are complex and multifaceted, it is useful to think of them as the six C's: Costs, Capital, Consumers, Climate, Consciousness, and Convergence.[13]

TABLE 1.1	Drivers of Opportunity—The Six C's	
Driver	*Description*	*Examples*
Costs	Declining costs of clean technology Increasing costs of natural resources Increasing internalization of externalities	Declining costs of wind power Increasing costs of oil Increasing costs of carbon emissions
Capital	Increasing investor and government funding of social and environmental enterprises	Clean-tech venture capital Social capital and impact investing Government stimulus packages aimed at green technology
Consumers	Increasing desire to purchase green products	Organic foods, fair-trade coffee, renewable energy
Climate	Global climate change	Carbon taxes and cap-and-trade regimes for greenhouse gas emissions
Consciousness	Increasing public awareness of environmental and social issues	Changing attitudes and beliefs about environmental effects and how those effects impact economic activity
Convergence	Increasing alignment between economic incentives and positive social and environmental outcomes	Increased regulation, market incentives, and stricter property rights for environmental resources such as fisheries

COSTS

The foremost trends in the green revolution can be seen in changing costs, and there are three important cost drivers for sustainable venturing in the world today: declining clean-technology costs, increasing natural resource costs, and increased internalization of environmental costs. First and perhaps most important, the cost of clean technology is falling rapidly. This is probably nowhere more evident than in the clean-energy sector. The cost of generating utility-scale wind power, for example, is now quite competitive with the production of electricity through the burning of coal. By building large farms of wind turbines, entrepreneurs have been able to substantially lower the costs of generating wind power. Second, the cost of resources is trending upward.[14] Though energy prices rise and fall with the global economy, many predict that the costs of fossil fuels will rise substantially over the next few decades. Increasing fossil fuel prices will make clean energy even more attractive, and will drive entrepreneurs to build more and more businesses that deliver products and services with minimal energy and resource use. Third, emerging national and international policies will increase the costs of doing business for those that harm the environment. Economists refer to this as *internalizing externalities,* which means that businesses that damage the environment will increasingly bear the burden of their actions in their bottom line. Together, these cost drivers are changing the competitive rules of the game, making sustainable entrepreneurship ever more attractive as clean technologies become more efficient, resource prices rise, and governments require producers to bear the full costs of their production.

CAPITAL

Private investors have determined that there is money to be made through sustainable venturing. Some investors who may see nothing but dollars are quite happy to participate in endeavors that help preserve our environment. Others are more driven by the prospect of social or ecological sustainability, but still care a great deal about their investments and returns. Private investors putting dollars into environmental ventures include venture capitalists, private equity firms, growth funds, corporations, angel investors, and a myriad of self-funded entrepreneurs. Venture capitalists invest in high-potential firms, typically those with new technologies. In the past decade, venture capital investment in the global clean technology sector rose from almost nothing to $8.9 billion in 2011.[15] Leading venture capital firms such as Khosla Ventures and Kleiner, Perkins Caufield and Byers (KPCB) have raised hundreds of million of dollars for specialized green investment funds and have been rapidly investing in emerging clean-tech companies. Expansion funds take these ventures to the next level, funding firms with proven technologies or products in need of growth financing. Individual angel investors typically fund environmental entrepreneurs in earlier stage companies with smaller investments. Large corporations such as Walmart, GE, and Sun Microsystems have been investing in both internal and external entrepreneurs with ideas for increased efficiency and enhanced sustainability. In total, global investment in clean energy was estimated to be $260 billion in 2011 (see Figure 1.1).

Governments are also getting into the act. National, state, and local governments have initiated a host of tax incentives, rebates, regulatory requirements, research programs, and even direct investments that financially support environmental entrepreneurs. Their motivations for such investments vary, but most programs are directed at promoting clean industries, creating employment opportunities, advancing energy independence and national security, or helping solve the climate change issue. Germany, for example, has led the world in support of rooftop solar electric systems through tariffs that return money to owners of the systems. By offering this support early, the German government has expedited the creation of a number of new companies that are leading the way in solar technology. State-level renewable portfolio standards in the United States require electric utilities to produce a certain percentage of their power from renewable sources. Such states have witnessed the proliferation of start-ups in the renewable energy market.[16]

CONSUMERS

Consumers have also been a driving force in the environmental entrepreneurship revolution. Across the world, consumers are demanding more accountability on

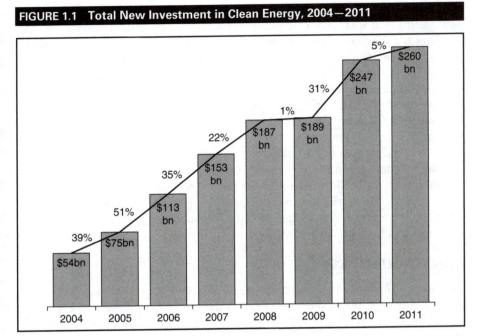

FIGURE 1.1   Total New Investment in Clean Energy, 2004—2011

Source: Bloomberg New Energy Finance: Green Investing 2011, Global Trends in Clean Energy Investment, 12 January 2012. Bloomberg, LP.

the part of producers, driving fundamental changes in behavior. *Negative screening* occurs when consumers avoid certain products or brands because of their environmental impact. Purchasing fair-trade coffee, renewable energy, or dolphin-safe tuna are prime examples of consumer purchasing decisions based on environmental factors. Some consumers are willing to pay more for environmentally differentiated products, potentially providing extra margins to the entrepreneurs who produce them. These consumers "vote with their wallet" to support their core beliefs and values. Companies like Renewable Choice, Green Mountain Coffee, and Terrapass have all benefited from these changing consumer behaviors. Other customers don't necessarily care about environmental impacts of products, but look for a host other benefits associated with these products. For example, the green building market has expanded rapidly, not so much because customers want a green building per se, but rather because they desire increased energy efficiency, lower toxicity, enhanced comfort, and greater workforce productivity. The same may be said for organic foods, as most customers purchase organic foods first and foremost because they are concerned about their, and their children's, health.

CLIMATE

Climate change is the most prevalent environmental issue in the world today. The idea that human burning of fossil fuels (coal, oil, and natural gas) could produce enough greenhouse gases to alter the climate was introduced decades ago. Scientists estimate with increasing certainty that the global climate is changing, that the change is caused by the human production of greenhouse gases, and that it will have substantial effects on our society and economy. While many wrestle over the science of climate change or agonize about its negative impacts, environmental entrepreneurs see an opportunity to use business as a vehicle for making positive environmental impact. Regardless of the arguments over the science, we are already in a system of increasing greenhouse gas management and control—what many call a "carbon-constrained world." What this means for business is an increasing "cost of carbon" wherein companies, and even individuals, pay for their greenhouse gas emissions. Such costs are changing the fundamental incentives in the marketplace so that clean, low-carbon technologies and products are more poised to win the competitive game. Innovative entrepreneurs recognize the value of low-carbon technologies and may sell their carbon credits on global and national carbon markets.

CONSCIOUSNESS

Fundamental changes in global consciousness with respect to environmental issues are driving sustainable venturing. At the foundation of this new consciousness is increasing scientific and popular knowledge about issues such as climate change, population growth, and ecological degradation. But this consciousness goes beyond just knowledge to changing values about what is important, appropriate, and rewarded in the economic system. While individual action is driven by the present system of rewards, future action is a function of the changing beliefs held by society, and those beliefs eventually impact the rules of the game in which entrepreneurs participate. The process of changing beliefs and attitudes and adjusting rules to match those beliefs is slow, but continuous. Beliefs tend to change over decades and sometime centuries, but they can also change rapidly, typically in response to a major event or crisis. Today, the tension between old ways of thinking about industry and the economy and emerging beliefs about the impact of our economy on the environment is evident to those with the awareness to see it. How rapidly the tension will break remains to be seen, but the convergence between new beliefs and the reality of our present ecological condition is already underway.

CONVERGENCE

Convergence is the increasing alignment between the institutions (or rules of the game) that determine competitive behavior and the modern realities of our planet. In other words, convergence is the increasing alignment between the nature of opportunity in our economic system and the creation of socially and ecologically sustainable value. As global consciousness of ecological degradation increases, the incentives for more sustainable action will grow, and capitalism will become increasingly aligned with good social and environmental outcomes. Such convergence is the locus of opportunity for entrepreneurial action, and the realm of the sustainable entrepreneur. Whether it is global climate change policy, tax credits for renewable energy, rising energy prices, or increasing recognition of the lower costs of sustainable technologies, entrepreneurs in the post-industrial world will be increasingly rewarded for their sustainable actions.

But the best sustainable entrepreneurs don't just wait for the convergence of economics incentives and ecological sustainability. Rather, they initiate the changes that help reward them for their more sustainable business models. They take it upon themselves to change the rules of the game in their favor and in favor of the environment. In the face of entrenched interests, this can be a difficult and time-consuming process, but the wind of sustainability and the societal value created by more sustainable business models can help entrepreneurs change the system of rewards. These entrepreneurs also find allies in the myriad of government agencies and nonprofits that share their visions and goals. Perhaps most important, their passion, belief, and action are critical elements in overcoming the status quo.

MYTHS ABOUT SUSTAINABLE VENTURING

The popularity of the concept of sustainable entrepreneurship is rapidly increasing. Indeed, many are excited about the prospect entrepreneurship holds for the environment. But many also misconceive what it is and how the process might work to help build a more sustainable economy. The following are common myths about sustainable entrepreneurship.

Myth 1: Sustainable venturing is about saving the world, not making a profit.

Doing the right thing and contributing to sustainability is the objective of many sustainable entrepreneurs, and their passion for implementing change can be a strong driving force for entrepreneurs, their employees, and their investors. But business activity that is not profitable is not economically sustainable, nor is it particularly replicable. There is probably no better motivation for entrepreneurs than to prove that you can make money while contributing to sustainability.

Myth 2: You have to want to save the world to be a sustainable entrepreneur.

Contrary to popular belief, not all sustainable entrepreneurs are passionate about resolving our environmental challenges. Some just see the business opportunities present in the transition to a sustainable economy and act more in response to profit signals than to a personal desire for change. If they are successful, the outcome can be similar, regardless of the initial motivation.

Myth 3: If I just do well for the environment, I'll make money.

Green is not always green. The reality of our current economic system is that many actions that would be helpful to the environment just aren't attractive from a business perspective, at least today. Some business ideas that are better for the environment will not yet be successful because they are not yet attractive economic opportunities. The key is to find where more sustainable business models intersect with the potential for profitability or to change the rules of the game to make it so.

Myth 4: Consumers will prefer my green product over less green options.

A percentage of consumers buy products because of their environmental values and are even willing to pay more. This represents a real green opportunity, although a niche one. Most customers care much more about product performance and quality. Sustainable entrepreneurs who wish to access broader markets need to provide and communicate a value proposition that goes beyond green. Fortunately, value drivers such as energy efficiency, healthfulness, and lower operating costs tend to be associated with green products. Selling these value attributes is usually the best way to market a green product or service.

Myth 5: Once I find the right environmental opportunity, the rest is easy.

The world will not beat a path to your door just because you build a better mousetrap. Sustainable entrepreneurship, like most entrepreneurial endeavors, requires good business strategy and effective implementation. You'll want a source of competitive advantage, like a good brand name, differentiated product, or intellectual property. The best sustainable entrepreneurs also attract teams of intelligent and experienced professionals who complement their skills. Starting a business is no easy matter, and sustainable entrepreneurs need to be prepared for the challenge.

THE DOMAINS OF SUSTAINABLE ENTERPRISE

As you learn more about sustainability and business, you will come across a variety of terms, and it is useful to understand the differences and similarities between them. In this process, it is important to recognize that many of the terms are just now emerging, and definitions are not always clear. In addition, the scope of issues and methodologies associated with sustainability in business is large, so there is a great deal of ground to cover. One way to think about the various terms is shown in Figure 1.2. The figure shows the overlapping domains of sustainable enterprise— sustainable venturing, social entrepreneurship, and corporate sustainable enterprise—illustrating how the concepts are related. *Corporate sustainable enterprise* tends to focus on the challenges and techniques of managing sustainability issues in large companies. Managing risks, measuring emissions and effects, and generating policies and systems to accommodate sustainability are foremost in the field of corporate sustainable enterprise. Both social entrepreneurship and sustainable venturing tend to focus more (though not exclusively) on innovative new organizations that solve social and environmental challenges. The field of *social entrepreneurship* emerged at least partially from nonprofit organizations, so there is a tendency to focus less on profit motivations and more on impact. In contrast, *sustainable venturing* (or entrepreneurship) is often more closely affiliated

FIGURE 1.2 Domains of Sustainable Enterprise

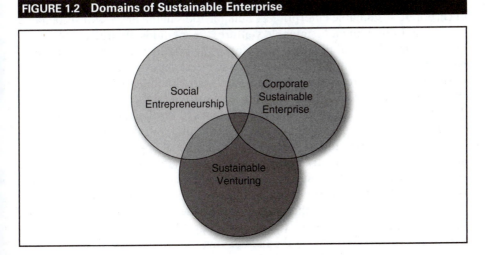

with market-driven enterprises and the increasing alignment between economic motivations and social and environmentally sustainable outcomes.

In addition, the term *social entrepreneurship* is popularly affiliated with enterprises that create (or desire to create) social value, whereas the term *sustainable entrepreneurship* is often associated with enterprises that reduce environmental degradation or improve ecological systems. Our perspective in this text is that the term *sustainability* encompasses social, environmental, and economic aspects. Perhaps most important, we believe that social and environmental issues are so intertwined that it is impossible to achieve sustainable development without considering both. Social problems can exacerbate environmental challenges as the poor struggle to survive and social systems fail to recognize the value of critical environmental resources. Conversely, environmental problems can have serious effects on social conditions, as natural resources necessary to support human populations degrade. The destruction of forests, for example, can cause desertification and flooding, as well as diminish food resources for local populations. Global climate change can have similar effects and can cause decreases in agricultural productivity. Such changes can result in armed conflict over resources and migrations that exacerbate social challenges. Furthermore, it is difficult to conceive of economically sustainable societies in which social or environmental problems are pervasive.

FOCUS OF THE BOOK

This book focuses on market-driven business ventures, which capture opportunities emerging from environmental challenges. We embrace the concept of social entrepreneurship as part of the domain of sustainable venturing, particularly for its unique focus on mission-driven organizations that have the potential to enhance both social and environmental sustainability. We also see the methods of corporate sustainable enterprise as valuable tools in the process of sustainable venturing. In building a sustainable venture, the methods of large corporations in addressing sustainability can be useful to the budding sustainable entrepreneur. Perhaps most important, we emphasize economic opportunities that are arising from the increasing challenges of a planet with limited resources. We see the sustainable entrepreneur and venture as responding to changing economic dynamics, using market-driven action as a means to resolve these challenges.

The next chapter provides an economic systems view of environmental challenges as a foundation for understanding the nature of opportunities for sustainable venturing. Chapter 3 translates some of these system-level perspectives into specific strategies that the sustainable entrepreneur can use to overcome barriers to the effective functioning of markets and to enable the sustainable venture. Chapter 4 focuses on the concept of social entrepreneurship, explaining the potential for entrepreneurs to solve social problems through mission-driven endeavors. Chapter 5 discusses the field of environmental marketing, addressing five opportunities to market products and services based on their environmental or social attributes. Chapter 6 then discusses the methods and considerations necessary to start and build the sustainable venture. Chapter 7 provides an overview of venture finance for the sustainable entrepreneur.

Summary

As our global society struggles with the challenges of environmental degradation and ecological sustainability, we increasingly look toward the process of entrepreneurship as the answer. Sustainable venturing holds the potential for innovative solutions to our most pressing challenges. The revolution of sustainable entrepreneurship is already underway, and there is much more to come as society adjusts to the reality of post-industrialism. The potential convergence between the creation of value for society in the realm of the environment and economic returns for entrepreneurs is what makes sustainable entrepreneurship one of the most exciting frontiers in today's world. Properly incentivized by the economic system, sustainable entrepreneurs can have their cake and eat it too. They can be passionate about resolving our environmental challenges and put profits in their pockets for their efforts.

Endnotes

1. Lea Goldman and Tom Post, "A Cry in the Wilderness," *Forbes* 165, no. 11(2000): 322–324.

2. G. Pascal Zachary, "Why the Soy Milk King Still Reigns," *Business 2.0* 5, no. 3 (April 2004): 73–74.

3. Craftskills, East Africa Limited, at http://craftskillseastafrica.com/b-one-default. html, accessed January 20, 2012.

4. J. Schmitt, "Craft Skills East Africa Limited," in T. J. Dean and M. D. M. Birnbaum, *Cases with a Conscience* (Boulder, CO: Sustainable Venturing Press, 2011).

5. Adam Smith, *The Wealth of Nations* (London: Strahan and Cadell, 1776), p. 456.
6. Steve Connor, "Forty Years Since the First Picture of Earth from Space," *The Independent*, January 10, 2009, available online at http://www.independent.co.uk/news/science/forty-years-since-the-first-picture-of-earth-from-space-1297569.html.
7. R. Costanza, R. d'Arge, R. de Groot, S, Farber, M. Grasso, B. Hannon, K. Limburg, S. Naeem, R. V. O'Neill, and J. Paruelo, "The Value of the World's Ecosystem Services and Natural Capital," *Nature* 387 (May 1997): 253–260.
8. M. Wackernagel and W. Rees, *Our Ecological Footprint: Reducing Human Impact on the Earth* (Gabriola Island, BC: New Society Publishers, 1996).
9. Redefining Progress website, http://rprogress.org/ecological_footprint/about_ecological_footprint.htm, accessed January 8, 2013.
10. G. Bruntland, ed. *Our common future: The World Commission on Environment and Development* (Oxford, Oxford University Press, 1987).
11. Francis Cairncross, *Costing the Earth: The Challenge for Governments, the Opportunities for Business* (Boston: Harvard Business School Press, 1992), p. 177.
12. "Used Cooking Oil Recycling," http://www.recycoil.com/ucor.html, accessed January 20, 2012.
13. Based on R. Pernick and C. Wilder, *The Clean Tech Revolution* (New York: Collins Business, 2008).
14. R. Dobbs, J. Oppenheim, and F. Thompson, "Mobilizing for a Resource Revolution," *McKinsey Quarterly* (January 2012): 1–15. Available online at https://www.mckinseyquarterly.com/Mobilizing_for_a_resource_revolution_2908.
15. Whitney Bennett Michael, "Corporate Cleantech M&A Grew 153 Percent in 2011 Totaling $41.2 Billion," press release, January 5, 2012, The Cleantech Group.
16. D. Yergin, *The Quest: Energy, Security, and the Remaking of the Modern World* (New York: Penguin, 2011).

CHAPTER 2

SYSTEMS AND OPPORTUNITIES

INTRODUCTION

In the first chapter, we learned that economic opportunities either exist within the system of rewards present in the economy at a given time or can be created through changes in the system of rewards within a reasonable period. In other words, the nature of incentives present or possible within an economy drives opportunities. Stated differently, the economic behaviors of individuals, corporations, and entrepreneurs are driven by the systems that reward them for various actions. The character of these rewards varies greatly and ranges from the prices of goods, to legal constraints, to social norms that dissuade certain behaviors or encourage others. The system of incentives (and disincentives) is generally referred as the *economic system*. This chapter considers a number of important points about economic systems, sustainability, and entrepreneurship.

First, it is useful to consider the underlying goal of an economic system and how we might gauge the difference between a good economic system and a bad one. Many think that the goal of an economic system is to make money and consider wealth generation as a proxy for success within an economy. But the generation of monetary wealth is at best an intermediate goal of economics. Money itself is no more useful than the paper on which it is printed. Money's potential translation into value is what matters. *The fundamental goal of an economic system is not to make money per se, but to provide value to members of society.* Economists refer to this as the *satisfaction of needs and wants*. The ultimate test of an economic system is the extent to which that system is providing value for members of the society that it serves. Value is also a humanly determined concept and rests in the minds of individuals. Economists, therefore, should be more concerned with whether a system effectively and efficiently helps individuals in a society to increase their utility and achieve their goals than with whether any particular product or service is produced.

Following on our discussion of Adam Smith's "invisible hand" in the first chapter, economic systems tend to be successful when they create win–win scenarios for their members. *Win–win* refers to conditions wherein the more an individual or organization does for society (the more value it creates), the more economically successful that individual or organization will become. Entrepreneurs, driven by win–win conditions in our capitalistic economic systems, have offered a plethora of rapid advances in medicine, transportation, communication, entertainment, and other fields. The "invisible hand" appears to work well in most domains. Indeed, writers are arguing it is increasingly possible for companies to *do well by doing good,* wherein doing well refers to making money, while doing good refers to solving some of our social and environmental challenges. Indeed, the popular literature on sustainable enterprise is rich with examples of win–win conditions in which companies pursued sustainable actions and became more profitable, either by increasing revenues or lowering costs. From green building to renewable energy to organic foods, entrepreneurs have found ways to make money with less social and environmental impact. The good news is that companies have created sustainable ventures that allow them to have a positive social or environmental impact while yielding economic returns. Economic growth through positive social and environmental business activity means everyone is better off. The idea that one can make the world a better place by employing business strategies and tactics, while at the same time enriching oneself, is a powerful concept.

Yet enthusiasm for win–win solutions must be tempered by the obvious social and environmental challenges that remain within our economic systems. From issues of climate change, freshwater shortages, degraded fisheries, and the loss of biodiversity, to persistent poverty and inequality, it is not at all clear that win–win solutions prevail in all contexts. Economist John Forbes Nash, Jr. (the subject of the film *A Beautiful Mind*), proposed equilibrium conditions under which competitive decisions result in a worse outcome for those engaged in the game, potentially contrary to the assumptions of the invisible hand.[1] A simplified version of this idea, applied to the realm of social and environmental outcomes in business, is that of *win–lose* conditions.[2] In other words, actions that might make a company more profitable may make society worse off (e.g., cause environmental degradation), or actions that would make society better off may reduce a company's profitability. The persistence of damaging environmental pollution and degradation suggest the persistence of such win–lose conditions.

Figure 2.1 divides the potential social and environmental activities of business into three categories. The first are *win–win* activities, which have already been discovered and implemented by businesses (*discovered win–win actions*) and offer private economic benefits and better social or environmental outcomes. These conditions represent potential opportunities but are relatively less interesting to the sustainable entrepreneur because they are already in widespread

FIGURE 2.1   Win–Win and Win–Lose Conditions

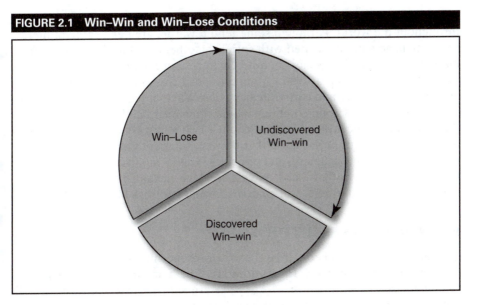

use and have little potential for superior economic return. The second category includes *win–win* conditions that are undiscovered or underexploited (*undiscovered win–win actions*). These conditions represent substantive opportunities for expanding actions that simultaneously reduce degradation or enhance social or environmental resources while offering the potential for superior profitability. Many of these are cataloged in popular books on sustainable enterprise and the subject of much discussion in later parts of this text. The third are *win–lose* conditions, which might offer the opportunity to enhance environmental outcomes, but are not incented by current market conditions. From an environmental and entrepreneurial perspective, these activities are perhaps the most intractable ones. But because they are the toughest nuts to crack, so to speak, they may offer the greatest economic returns, if the market conditions on which they are based are changing or may be altered by entrepreneurial action. The transformation of win–lose conditions to win–win conditions is of great interest to the environmental entrepreneur. The transformation from win–lose conditions rests in changes to the market institutions that create economic incentives.[3] Understanding the nature of these institutions is the topic of the remainder of this chapter and the next.

ECONOMIC SYSTEMS AND INSTITUTIONS

Economic systems exist within, and are a fundamental part of, broader social systems. Stated differently, *economic systems are embedded within social systems* and the associated norms, values, beliefs, priorities, and legal structures of those social systems. This helps account for the vast differences in economic systems throughout the world. Although some tend toward a greater degree of hierarchical management associated with socialism, others tend toward a more free-market orientation. Regardless of a system's economic philosophy (e.g., socialist or capitalist), systems may also vary in the specific rules and rights that govern and drive competitive and corporate behavior. Whether it is tax policies, rules of incorporation, or environmental regulation, companies in different societies face different sets of incentives and constraints. Economic systems are embedded within social systems in the sense that they are inherently driven by the nature of social norms, values, beliefs, and priorities. This is important to entrepreneurs because, to the extent that social systems drive the economic systems of rewards, entrepreneurial opportunity will be driven by the priorities of social systems.

ECONOMIC INSTITUTIONS

The term used to broadly describe the drivers of incentives and rewards in society is *economic institutions*. Institutions are "the humanly devised constraints that shape human interaction."[4] They are argued to "structure incentives in human exchange, whether political, social, or economic"[5] and therefore serve as the central driver of economic activity and development.[6] They are, in essence, the rules of the game by which economic actors play. Institutions are not, as most people think, specific organizations, but rather the underlying structures on which those organizations are founded. Primary examples of economic institutions that are important to entrepreneurs include the granting of legal status to corporations, the system of property rights by which individuals own land and products, and the legal frameworks of intellectual property protection (like patents). Institutions can range from highly formalized structures, such as laws, to informal customs and values, such as a handshake agreement or cultural acceptance of innovative behavior. Both formal and informal institutions govern how people and organizations act and the rewards resulting from various actions.

Patent law is probably the best example of the role of economic institutions with respect to entrepreneurs and the returns to innovation. Patent laws vary from country to country, but generally speaking, patent laws grant temporary exclusive right to commercial use of a novel product or technology. Patent laws allow holders of patents to sue companies that infringe on their intellectual property, and such laws are important to economic development and social value creation. By granting exclusive rights to innovators, society increases entrepreneurs' potential return to innovation and society gains from increases in the rate of innovation. As a result, the institution of patent law helps drive innovation and entrepreneurship.

Formal rights to real estate are another important example of the role of economic institutions. A system of legal rights to land ownership and use creates incentives to invest in assets on property because it secures future ownership of those investments. Moreover, in most nations individuals can borrow capital against their real assets and employ that capital to create additional value in society. In the absence of such property rights, land stewardship can suffer, and individuals have very few means of unlocking opportunities to borrow capital against their real assets, further perpetuating the cycle of poverty. In the book *The Mystery of Capital,* Hernando de Soto argues that the lack of formal property rights for land in underdeveloped countries has been one of the primary reasons that those countries have been unable to emerge from poverty.[7] DeSoto also emphasizes the absence of individual legal identity, bureaucratic barriers to company formation, and other institutional failures that prevent the accumulation of capital and inhibit entrepreneurial behavior. Because of the tremendous impact economic institutions have on society's ability to generate wealth, they are indeed a major consideration for entrepreneurs seeking opportunities in various political regimes and economic systems.

Economic historian Douglass North was awarded the Nobel Prize in economics for his work on the link between economic institutions and economic development.[8] He argues that economic development in Western economies over the past centuries resulted directly from the development of new institutions that encouraged productive entrepreneurial endeavors. North emphasizes how new institutions develop over time, particularly in the long-term. Again, patent law is an instructive example, as it shows how the development of economic institutions effect economic development over the long run. The history of patents goes back as far as ancient Greece, but the first formal patent law was not put into place until the 1400s in the Republic of Venice.

Thus, environmental entrepreneurship rests on the principles that *economic systems and institutions are in a continual state of change* and that *the manner in which economic institutions are evolving is at least partially in response to the emerging needs of society and the increasing scarcity of resources.* As Douglass North and Robert Thomas explain,

> Economic institutions, and specifically property rights, are generally considered by economists as parameters; but for the study of long-term economic growth, they are clearly variables, historically subject to fundamental change.[9]

Economic institutions need not be laws and regulations monitored and enforced by the government. Institutions can also be cultural, tied to the social norms of the community. For example, certain tasks or jobs may only be restricted to those of a particular gender, race, or class. Religion is another important institution that influences the way in which a society conducts business. Knowing and understanding how different societies and cultures operate is imperative to the sustainable entrepreneur. Even if the endeavor is completely legal, yields a positive impact, and can generate profit, if it goes against a deep seeded cultural institution, it may never get off the ground because the community cannot or will not support it.

ECO-INSTITUTIONAL CONVERGENCE

Eco-institutional convergence is the idea that economic institutions are evolving in response to fundamental ecological challenges and that, as a result, entrepreneurs will be increasingly incented to resolve these ecological challenges. In other words, the nature of economic institutions will evolve and converge with the need for the resolution of global ecological challenges. But most important, as these changes alter the rules of the game in competitive markets, they create economic opportunity for businesses that create sustainable economic and environmental value.

New institutions driving market opportunities in environmental entrepreneurship have been emerging rapidly in the past decades. They range from voluntary industry labeling initiatives, to international policy agreements, to new market mechanisms for trading pollution credits. Such developments need not be driven by government legislation. Individuals or groups with an interest in environmental sustainability or economic profit may also create new institutions in a voluntary manner. Institutional changes driven by legislation also need not be regulatory, as a host of other policies drive economic behavior. Alternatives to command-and-control regulations include new property rights, certification and labeling schemes, disclosure requirements, deposit-refund schemes, new market mechanisms, pollution taxes, and alternative subsidies. Finally, eco-institutional convergence may be driven as much from the bottom-up as it is from the top–down.

Further understanding of the nature of eco-institutional convergence and the opportunities created by this convergence can be gained by understanding current and historical imperfections in our market institutions, as those imperfections are seen as largely responsible for our environmental challenges.

MARKET FAILURES

The field of *environmental economics* is concerned with whether market systems are effective and efficient in allocating environmental resources, and if not, what might be done about it. Environmental economists approach *environmental challenges primarily as an economic problem*. In other words, they trace the source of environmental challenges back to the economic system and ask how the economic system has resulted in our modern environmental problems and/or how it might solve them. The concept of *market failure* is one of the most prevalent concepts in the field, as market failure is largely viewed as the economic cause of environmental degradation. Market failure can be viewed as the *inability of a system of market institutions to incent desirable activities or impede undesirable ones.*[10] Market failures are, in essence, conditions that drive entrepreneurs and businesses to make win–lose decisions (win for the company, but lose for society). They are called *market failures* because the system incents a suboptimal outcome. In other words, in such situations a corporation or entrepreneur pursues its own self-interest to the detriment to society at large. The market is failing to provide the most effective or efficient solution.

Market failures that have negative impacts on environmental resources have been termed *environmentally relevant market failures.*[11] Environmentally relevant market failures are particularly prevalent because many environmental resources, such as the atmosphere, have characteristics that make them less amenable to market allocation.[12] Air and water, for example, can be difficult resources to manage through market systems because they tend to be transient and indivisible.[13] It is also the case that many of these resources have been abundant in the past, but are just now becoming scarce. As scarcity increases, the inability of our market system to effectively value and steward environmental and natural resources has become more obvious and more problematic. This condition is popularly referred to as *the tragedy of the commons,* a situation in which individuals collectively engage in depleting a shared resource because each individual is acting in his or her own best interest in the short term, even though it is in no one's best interest in the long run.[14]

The existence of environmentally relevant market failures detracts from the sustainability of an economic system by allowing the degradation of the natural assets that are necessary to generate future economic value.[15] One way to understand market failures is through the concepts of *social costs and private costs.*[16] Social costs represent all of the costs of an activity incurred by the entirety of a society. They are typically contrasted with *private costs,* which are the costs borne by the individual or organization involved in an activity or transaction. Where social costs are greater than private costs, the individual or organization performing an activity does not bear all of the costs of that activity. For example, when coal is burned to create electricity, emissions containing particulates, sulfur dioxides, carbon dioxides, and mercury are released into the atmosphere. Unless required to eliminate these emissions or otherwise compensate society, the electric utility does not bear the costs of the emissions. But society does, because those emissions affect health, agricultural productivity, and ecosystems downwind of the utility. Such costs are often referred to as *external costs,* because they exist external to the party that created them, which does not pay for them.

From a systems perspective, the presence of social costs above and beyond private costs (often referred to as *external costs* or *negative externalities*) creates perverse market incentives that are of particular concern for the efficient functioning of an economic system, and by extension the proper allocation of resources. If, for example, utilities do not pay the full costs of production from coal, the dynamics of supply and demand suggest that society ends up with higher production of electricity from coal than might otherwise be ideal. Where substantial external costs of an activity exist, an industry or a producer is in essence "subsidized" because it does not have to pay the full costs of that productive activity. From an entrepreneurial perspective, the ability to externalize costs on others makes the production of electricity from coal relatively more attractive than the production of electricity from other energy sources, such as wind or solar power, because the electricity entrepreneur choosing to use coal does not have to pay the full costs of power generation.

Market failures may also occur from the creation of *social benefits* that do not accrue to the individual or organization engaged in that activity. One classic example of external benefit occurs in vaccinations. Social benefits from an individual receiving a vaccination for a communicable disease accrue to others in society because the vaccination reduces the probability of others getting the disease (in addition to reducing the probability of the individual acquiring the disease). Because individuals are not necessarily willing to pay to prevent others from getting a disease, it is often suggested that the market system will result in fewer vaccinations than what would be ideal from society's perspective. Social benefits above private benefits are referred to as *external benefits* or *positive externalities.* Industries or companies producing positive external benefits for which they are not rewarded will tend to be relatively less incented to produce their product or service. Most important, an entrepreneur who is unable to capture all of the benefits of a product or service is less likely to offer that product or service. So the entrepreneur must find a way through the current system of rewards, or by altering the system of rewards, to capitalize on all of the benefits they create for society.

The ability of an entrepreneur to *appropriate* the returns from the benefits created by its activity is important in the effective functioning of a market system, as well as to the viability of an entrepreneurial endeavor. Likewise, the ability to require producers to pay the full costs of their activities is important for market systems and for the ability of entrepreneurs with environmentally superior business models and technologies to be successful. If external costs and benefits are not borne by the producer of goods or services, the system of rewards may be incenting suboptimal economic performance. In other words, there are dormant opportunities waiting to be exploited by the entrepreneur who can find a way to successfully navigate the system.

The *polluter pays principle,* supported by the Organization for Economic Cooperation and Development, states that polluters should bear the full costs of any damage caused by their production of goods and services. If the full costs of damages to society are integrated into the production of pollution-generating goods or services, the prices to consumers may rise, making cleaner substitutes more economically viable and attractive to the consumer.

Consistent with the polluter pays principle, *full-cost pricing* exists when prices reflect all of the costs of production, including the costs of environmental degradation and negative social impacts. Full-cost pricing enables sustainable development through a free-market system because prices are a more accurate reflection of the resources necessary to produce a given product or service. In such a scenario, environmentally or socially harmful activities look relatively less attractive in the marketplace than those that do not create such damages, because customers face a relatively lower price for the less damaging products or services. The goal, then, from a systems perspective, is that market failures remain relatively minimal, and private costs and benefits be approximate to social costs and benefits. While there are substantive efforts to achieve full-cost pricing in our economic system, most observers suggest that prices still do not reflect many of the social and environmental damages of some productive activities.

MARKET FAILURE AS ENTREPRENEURIAL OPPORTUNITY

Understanding market failure is central to understanding the potential economic opportunities available in environmental entrepreneurship for two reasons. First, the magnitude of *potential* opportunities for sustainable venturing corresponds to the level of market failure and to the value being lost to society because of the degradation of environmental resources. To the extent that environmental degradation results in diminished ecosystem services, social value can be obtained by preserving or enhancing the resources affected, meaning that entrepreneurs who can capture some of the value created through the preservation or betterment of the natural resources can start profitable ventures. We are beginning to see this phenomenon occur in and around many ecosystem services. Watershed protection is one that is of particular importance in the western United States. Private companies and governments are increasingly willing to pay for the availability of clean water from a natural source (e.g., streams, rivers, or lakes). By paying someone to protect the watershed from which the water is generated, the company is better off, and the entity providing the service of maintaining the watershed has a revenue-generating opportunity. When considering the level of degradation in various ecosystems, the value that can be captured by such activities can be substantial.

Second, to the degree that we can understand the market failures preventing the efficient use of environmental resources, we can gauge the means by which entrepreneurs might resolve those failures and help preserve environmental resources. Biofuels can replace fossil fuels with less harmful alternatives. Biofuels become more economically viable when consumers of fossil fuels are required to pay the external costs of burning them. By working with the institutional framework to make such a switch economically viable for both the consumer and the producer, an entrepreneur can put resources to greater and better use while preserving natural resources and promoting environmental stewardship. Understanding how to build and/or exploit opportunities in eco-institutional convergence is a central strategy of sustainable venturing.

It is important to note that many market failures do not permanently exist within the economic system, nor does the market create them, per se; in other words, the term *market failure* is somewhat misleading. Many market failures result from the regulatory or legal environment put in place by the institutional actors within the economic system, while others are a result of society's norms, values, and traditions, all of which can change and evolve over time. Regardless of the reason for market failures, one should not assume that a market failure is permanent.

PLACES TO INTERVENE IN A SYSTEM

The above discussions are meant to make an important point about economic systems, sustainability, and entrepreneurial opportunity: that it is not always sufficient to take the system or the rules of the game as they are. Rather, much of sustainable

FIGURE 2.2 Places to Intervene in a System

Places to Intervene in a System, Revisited

Level	Frequency	Comments
Embeddedness: Norms, values, customs, beliefs, traditions, religion	100–1000 years Dynamics of punctuated equilibrium	What we believe Often non-calculative
Institutional Environment: Rules of the game, esp. politics, property rights, governance, judiciary, bureaucracy	10–100 years	Get the institutional environment right
Plays of the Game: Individual and organizational decisions and actions	Continuous	Short term action determined by incentives

Source: Williamson, O. 2000. The New Institutional Economics: Staking Stock, Looking Ahead. Journal of Economic Literature. Vol XXXVII September: 595–613. D. Meadows, "Leverage Points: Places to Intervene in a System," Solutions 1, no. 1(2009): 41–49, available online at http://www.thesolutionsjournal.com/node/419.

venturing is about changing the system to achieve better results and enable a new venture. System thinker and sustainable-development advocate Dana Meadows usefully summarizes this fact in her writings on "places to intervene in a system."[17] Figure 2.2 combines her approach with that of economist Oliver Williamson[18] to emphasize the hierarchy of leverage points in an economic system. The figure shows three levels of a system: the *plays of the game,* the *institutional environment,* and *embeddedness.* The *plays of the game* are decisions and actions made by individuals and organizations, including entrepreneurs. The institutional environment consists of the rules of the game by which such decisions are made, including the legal structures, property rights, political systems, and other formal and informal rules that determine the payoffs (or incentives) for various decisions and actions. At the highest level is embeddedness, which consists of the norms, values, customs, and beliefs that determining the nature of the rules and associated incentive structures.

Dana Meadows has pointed to the fact that the most effective place to alter a system is at the highest level, that of the embeddedness. This is because changes to norms, values, and beliefs affect the entire system. In other words, changes in embedded norms can alter the institutional environment, which then impacts individual decisions. In short, if you want to have the greatest impact on sustainable development, change what people believe and value. Unfortunately, the time frame for changing such beliefs is long, arguably in the range of centuries. Fortunately, beliefs can also change rapidly, often in response to an external event or occurrence. The dynamics of periods of little change, interspersed by rapid revolutionary change, are known as *punctuated equilibrium*. The next most-influential place to intervene in a system is at the institutional level, a dynamic discussed extensively above. In short, entrepreneurs have the opportunity to change the rules of the game in a way that enhances sustainability by increasing the incentives for more sustainable business models. We'll address the specifics of such actions (institutional strategies) in the next chapter. For now, the most important point is that sustainable entrepreneurs have the opportunity both to act within existing systems and to act on existing beliefs and institutions in order to enable their ventures. The best results may be achieved by operating on the latter of these, where potential leverage in the system is at its greatest, even though such changes may be the most difficult.

CLOSING THOUGHTS: GREAT CAPITALISM IS GREAT ENVIRONMENTALISM

Many argue that the cause of our environmental challenges and ecological unsustainability is a system of markets and government policies that sacrifice our longerterm environmental and economic health for current economic gains. Sometimes it seems that business enterprises are more motivated to pollute and diminish our natural resources than to enhance, or at least sustain, them. Capitalism, for all its benefits, may be eating at the very foundation upon which it is based, the ecological systems from which social wealth and value is ultimately derived. Such conditions have caused many environmentalists to question the value of capitalism and even to suggest that it be replaced with less market-oriented economic systems. But such approaches fail to understand the capacity of markets and entrepreneurship to help resolve our environmental ills and to build a more sustainable economy. Rejecting capitalism because of our ecological challenges would certainly be shortsighted. On the other hand, ignoring our current environmental challenges and the unwanted effects of our economic activity is equally inadvisable.

The key is to make markets and capitalism work for the environment rather than against it. Such an approach can capture the powerful benefits of capitalism and entrepreneurship while helping resolve our environmental challenges. As industrialist Stephan Schmidheiny has said, "The cornerstone of sustainable development is a system of open, competitive markets in which prices are made to reflect the cost of environmental as well as other resources."[19] According to this line of thought, *great capitalism is great environmentalism, and great environmentalism is great capitalism.*

Great capitalism as great environmentalism is closely aligned with the concept of *free-market environmentalism*. Free-market environmentalism emphasizes the role that properly structured markets and decentralized decision-making can play in effectively allocating natural and environmental resources.[20] Free-market environmentalism assumes that (1) individuals have a tendency to make decisions in their self-interest, (2) decentralized markets are better allocators of resources than centralized planning systems or political hierarchies, and

(3) well-specified property rights for environmental and natural resources will internalize costs of production and create a system in which prices will represent full costs. Most important, free-market environmentalism emphasizes the role that properly structured market systems can play in motivating innovative entrepreneurial solutions to environmental challenges.

Yet, it is not entirely clear how far a market-based approach can go in preserving certain ecological resources. While the purpose of this book is to emphasize market solutions and the opportunities available in the restructuring of market incentives, markets are nonetheless still a human tool, and thereby serve human wants and needs. Many environmentalists see ecological resources as having value that transcends their worth to human populations, a view typically known as *ecocentrism*. According the Food and Agriculture Organization of the United Nations *environmental resources* have an intrinsic value of their own, as well as of value for the longer-term use by human populations.[21] Yet only humans operate in markets and political systems, so free-market environmentalism and market-based approaches succeed only in so far as humans value environmental resources. Nevertheless, there is little doubt that we can go much further in aligning our market systems with the human value of ecological resources and thereby act to better sustain them.

Central to great capitalism and great environmentalism is a system of rewards that encourage ecologically sustainable entrepreneurial action. One of the most compelling management articles is Stephen Kerr's "On the Folly of Rewarding A While Hoping for B," in which the author points out the basic truism that "Whether dealing with monkeys, rats, or human beings, it is hardly controversial to state that most organisms seek information concerning what activities are rewarded, and then seek to do those things, often to the virtual exclusion of activities not rewarded."[22] And so it is with entrepreneurs: if our markets do not reward our entrepreneurs for protecting and enhancing our environmental resources and natural capital, they will not do so, and it is really quite difficult to blame them for that.

Conversely, if our markets *do* reward entrepreneurs for more sustainable enterprise, they will race to the decisions and actions that enhance sustainability, and the sustainable behaviors they pursue will be replicated across the world, whether or not each entrepreneur is passionate about saving the planet. Thus, the alignment of economic opportunity and entrepreneurial self-interest with ecologically sustainable outcomes is the goal of great capitalism and great environmentalism, and this alignment is the foundation upon which environmental entrepreneurs are changing our world and will pioneer a more sustainable future.

Key Learnings

1. The ultimate goal of an economic system is to provide value for its constituents. Better economic systems provide greater value for society.
2. *Win–win* situations occur when actions that benefit an individual or organization also benefit society—that is, when self-interest is aligned

with social value creation. Win–win situations are common and one of the primary benefits of the capitalistic economic system.

3. *Win–lose* situations exist when the pursuit of self-interest comes at the expense of society.

4. Win–win and win–lose conditions are determined by the nature of institutions in place within an economic system.

5. Institutions are the ways of doing things and rules of the game that create incentives in the economic system.

6. Institutions evolve over time, at least partially in response to emerging needs of society. *Eco-institutional convergence* refers to the way that institutions change in response to social and environmental challenges.

7. New, changing, or emerging institutions create opportunities for entrepreneurs.

8. Sustainable entrepreneurs can intervene in the system by creating new institutions that create win–win conditions and enhance sustainability. Intervening at the systems level can be difficult, but can also provide the greatest potential for impact.

9. *Market failures* are incidences in the economic system that create win–lose conditions. Many market failures occur with respect to environmental resources.

10. Market failures may be seen as potential opportunities for the sustainable entrepreneur.

Endnotes

1. J. Nash, "Non-cooperative Games," *Annals of Mathematics* 54 (1951): 286–295.
2. D. F. Pacheco, T. J. Dean, and D. S. Payne, "Escaping the Green Prison: Entrepreneurship and the Creation of Opportunities for Sustainable Development," *Journal of Business Venturing* 25 no. 5 (2010): 464–480.
3. Ibid.
4. D. C. North, *Institutions, Institutional Change, and Economic Performance* (Cambridge: Cambridge University Press, Cambridge, 1990), p. 3.
5. Ibid.
6. E. G. Furubotn and S. Pejovich, "Property Rights and Economic Theory: A Survey of Recent Literature," *Journal of Economic Literature* 10, no. 4 (1972), 1137–1162; D. W. Bromley, *Economic Interests and Institutions* (New York: Basil Blackwell, 1989).
7. H. DeSoto, "The Mystery of Capital," *Finance and Development* 38, no. 1:29-34.
8. D. C. North and R. P. Thomas, R.P., "An Economic Theory of the Growth of the Western World," *Economic History Review* 23, no. (1970): 1–17.
9. Ibid.
10. F. M. Bator, F.M., "The Anatomy of Market Failure, *Quarterly Journal of Economics* 72 (August 1958): 351–379; 351.
11. T. J. Dean and J. McMullen, "Toward a Theory of Sustainable Entrepreneurship: Reducing Environmental Degradation through Entrepreneurial Action," *Journal of Business Venturing* 22, no. 1 (2007): 50–76.
12. R. Dorfman, "Some Concepts from Welfare Economics," in *Economics of the Environment: Selected Readings*, ed. R. Dorfman and N. S. Dorfman (New York: W.W. Norton, 1993): 79–96.

13. Ibid.

14. G. Hardin, "The Tragedy of the Commons," *Journal of Science* 162 (1968):1243–1247.

15. Dean and J. McMullen, "Toward a Theory of Sustainable Entrepreneurship: Reducing Environmental Degradation through Entrepreneurial Action."

16. A. C. Pigou, *The Economics of Welfare*, 4th ed. (London: Macmillan, 1932).

17. D. Meadows, "Leverage Points: Places to Intervene in a System," *Solutions* 1, no. 1 (2009): 41–49, available online at http://www.thesolutionsjournal.com/node/419.

18. Oliver E. Williamson, "The New Institutional Economics: Taking Stock, Looking Ahead," *Journal of Economic Literature* 38, no. 3 (September 2000): 595–613.

19. S. Schmidheiny, *Changing Course: a Global Business Perspective on Development and the Environment* (Cambridge, MA: MIT Press, 1990), p. 14.

20. T. L. Anderson and D. R. Leal, *Free Market Environmentalism* (New York: Palgrave, 2001).

21. Land and Water Development Division of the Food and Agricultural Organization of the United Nations, "Planning for the Sustainable Use of Land Resources, Towards a New Approach," *FAO Land and Water Bulletin* 2 (1995).

22. S. Kerr, "On the Folly of Rewarding A, While Hoping for B," *Academy of Management Executive* 9, no. 1 (1995): 7–14, 7.

INSTITUTIONAL STRATEGIES FOR SUSTAINABLE VENTURING

INTRODUCTION

In the last chapter, we discussed economic systems and their role in motivating, or dissuading entrepreneurial action. The basic contention was that, with respect to natural and environmental resources, conditions of market failures could prevent entrepreneurs from implementing businesses that enhance ecological or social sustainability. In addition, we noted that conditions of market failure can be, and are being, altered through the processes of eco-institutional convergence. We also suggested that market failures are, at their essence, sources of entrepreneurial opportunity. In other words, win–lose conditions can be translated into win–win conditions through entrepreneurial action.

Environmental entrepreneurs engage in the processes of *opportunity recognition* and/or *opportunity creation* with respect to the institutional changes associated with eco-institutional convergence.[1] *Opportunity recognition* refers to the ability of entrepreneurs to perceive market gaps or imperfections within the economic systems — those that, if pursued, provide the potential for economic returns. Opportunity recognition within environmental entrepreneurship involves recognizing trends in eco-institutional convergence. For example, as governments continue to tighten regulations on the amount of greenhouse gas emissions that companies can produce, an opportunity lies in understanding what the regulations will mean to private industries, particularly those that are heavy polluters, and in creating a solution that allows them to lower greenhouse gas emissions through new technology or means of production. Helping industries to comply with upcoming regulations while making their operation more efficient and profitable is a win–win scenario. In short, environmental entrepreneurs can benefit from understanding how market institutions are changing for valuable natural and environmental resources like air, water, climate, and ecosystem services.

Opportunity creation refers to entrepreneurial actions that alter market systems to open up new opportunities for economic return. Opportunity creation in environmental entrepreneurship involves creating eco-institutional convergence by intervening in the system. In other words, the entrepreneur is proactively engaged in altering market institutions in a way that aligns ecological goals or outcomes with economic return. Entrepreneurs can create new market institutions and incentive systems that enable profitability for more environmentally friendly business strategies, models, technologies, and products. While there is no single right way to go about creating opportunities, there are indeed strategies to explore when developing a sustainable venture.

The strategies for opportunity recognition and creation in environmental entrepreneurship are varied, but recent history suggests that many strategies have proven successful. The key to understanding how to see or unlock emerging opportunities for environmental entrepreneurship rests in understanding the existing barriers to efficient markets.[2] In other words, the key to environmental entrepreneurship rests in understanding market failures in the current economic system. Later, we review the five institutional strategies that entrepreneurs can pursue to resolve the various types of market failure. We also distinguish between the institutional strategies and general business strategies, because institutional strategies alter institutional frameworks to enable sustainable ventures by addressing the market failures found within the system.

These institutional strategies are summarized in Table 3.1.

STRATEGY #1: DEFINE AND ENFORCE PROPERTY RIGHTS

The *property rights entrepreneur* implements new means of defining or enforcing property rights in order to enable a profitable venture.[3, 4] A *property right* is the authority to determine how a resource or asset is used. Property rights can apply to real estate (like land and its improvements), products (like cars and TVs), natural resources (like underground minerals), or intangible assets (like various forms intellectual property).

The purchase of a product, or other asset, is perhaps best conceived of as a purchase of a bundle rights, rather than as a purchase of a physical asset,[5] because physical assets and products come with a set of rights associated with them. Those rights may be broad and encompassing, or they may be constrained by legal structures or contracts. For example, rights to the minerals under housing subdivisions (i.e., oil or gold) are often not included with the right to occupy and build a house on the land. In subsidized housing, property buyers often relinquish their right to resell their property at market rates in return for a lower price when the house is purchased. Property rights may include a mix of the rights to (1) *possess* an asset,

TABLE 3.1 Institutional Strategies for Sustainable Venturing

Institutional Strategy	Entrepreneur	Action	Example
1. Define and Enforce Property Rights	Property rights entrepreneur	Establish excludability for asset, product, or service	Cap-and-Trade systems for greenhouse gas emissions
2. Internalize Externalities	Institutional Entrepreneur	Develop new economic institutions to eliminate externalities	Carbon taxes, regulations, and voluntary industry standards
3. Develop Informational Structures	Informational Entrepreneur	Develop systems to enhance information in markets	Green certification and labeling systems (Energy Star, organic foods, green building)
4. Transform Government Intervention	Political Entrepreneur	Motivate changes to taxes, subsidies, or other government incentives	Renewable energy feed—in tariffs and production tax credits Elimination of fossil fuel subsidies
5. Break Monopoly Power	Market-Appropriating Entrepreneur	Destroy monopolistic positions through new technology or deregulation	Deregulation of telecommunications industry, Net metering policies for electric utilities

(2) *utilize* an asset, (3) *exclude* others from its use, (4) *obtain a stream of income* from the asset, and/or 5) *transfer* (sell) the rights to others.[6–8]

Rights may be owned by states (*public property*) or by private individuals or organizations (*private property*). *Common property* refers to property that is held in common by a group or subset of individuals or organizations. Certain assets or resources may also not be subject to any ownership, with property rights to them undetermined or nonexistent. Property without defined rights is known as *open-access,* since use is open to all. Wildlife, for example, is often considered as being unowned. Property in the *public domain* may be seen as open-access, since all members of society may use it. The writings of Shakespeare, for example, exist in the public domain and may be copied and used by members of a society. In contrast, writings of more recent authors may be copyrighted and therefore exist as private property. Finally, property rights may be informal, meaning that they are not codified in law, contract, or written title, but are nonetheless recognized by certain groups.[9]

Good property rights regimes tend to make markets work effectively. For example, copyright law allows authors and musicians to benefit economically from their work, and therefore encourages the development of new works that provide entertainment and insight. Property rights work in markets because they provide *excludability,* meaning that owners of an asset can prevent others from using it (i.e., those who do not pay to use it).[10] In contrast, poorly defined or enforced property rights regimes can cause markets to fail or to operate suboptimally. The inability to prevent users from copying movies, for example, can reduce marginal returns to studios and diminish incentives for the production of new movies. The inability to *enforce* property rights can result in similar outcomes, rendering property rights effectively nonexistent. With movies, for example, the ability of consumers to make illegal digital copies without penalty may result in the same outcome as the lack of copyright laws: reduced returns and diminished incentives for production.

Poorly defined or enforced property rights regimes for natural and environmental resources are arguably one of the root causes of environmental degradation.[11] Compared to property rights for products and capital assets, property rights regimes for air, water, and other natural capital are often underdeveloped. The best example of a resource with little property right protection may be the high seas. Under the United Nations' Law of the Sea, individual countries maintain territorial waters and an exclusive economic zone, which extends up to 212 miles beyond their shore. Each country has an exclusive right to use these zones for various economic purposes, including tourism, fishing, oil production, or wind-power generation. International policy prevents foreign countries from exploiting economic resources in these zones, and individual nations who own them can implement policies to preserve the resources within them. Beyond this 212-mile limit, however, no particular individual or nation owns the high seas. While some constraints exist in international agreements, the high seas have a tendency to be over-fished because there is little regulation, and individual fishers have little motivation to leave breeding stocks in place (they likely assume that if they don't harvest the fish, someone else will). In short, the outcome of the lack of ownership of resources on the high seas can be detrimental to important economic resources, like fisheries.

This result of poorly defined or enforced property rights is popularly known as the *tragedy of the commons*,[12] a concept briefly mentioned in the previous chapter. The tragedy of the commons may result when a resource is unowned and access to it is unconstrained.[13] The analogy typically used to illustrate the tragedy of the commons is that of a common cattle pasture in villages. Each villager who has access to the commons is motivated to place more cattle on the pasture, because doing so increases his or her returns. But this occurs at the expense of the common good because, as each villager adds more cattle, the grass may die, and the land's ability to support cattle degrades. The tragedy of the commons occurs because no mechanism exists for excludability, and because the commons is *rivalrous*. Rivalry refers to the fact that one person's use of a product or asset diminishes or precludes another person's ability to use that same product or asset. The meaning of rivalry becomes more obvious when one thinks about *nonrival goods,* such as a digital musical recording, which can be listened to by numerous individuals in multiple locations without diminishing the quality of the recording or the ability of any of them to listen to it.

Goods that are nonexcludable and rivalrous (as in the tragedy of commons) are often referred to as *common goods* (despite the fact that it is their open-access [not common ownership] that creates the problem). Goods that are nonexcludable and nonrivalrous are known as *public goods.* Many people have historically referred to the air as a public good. While this is probably no longer the case (due to large-scale air pollution), air used to be considered a public good because individuals largely cannot be excluded from breathing it, and one individual's breathing does not materially diminish another person's ability to breathe. A *congestible good* is one that is nonrival at low levels of use, but becomes rivalrous at higher levels of use. Typical examples of congestible goods are national parks and highways. When highways are largely empty, adding another vehicle does not diminish the experience for other drivers. But when highways are congested, adding another vehicle can impact the speed of the traffic and diminish the experience of other drivers. Likewise, when national parks are relatively empty, the presence of other tourists has little effect on the aesthetics of the experience. But as the park becomes more crowded, the aesthetic experience can decline substantially from traffic congestion and noise.[14]

Nonexcludability in rivalrous goods creates two primary economic problems. The first is that nonexcludability can result in overuse (as in the tragedy of the commons analogy). The American bison, which roamed North America in millions, nearly became extinct because excludability was not established through ownership or other means. The second problem is that entrepreneurs will be less motivated to produce goods for which they cannot exclude nonpayers. Intellectual property right laws (patents and copyrights) were developed to change this dynamic and provide excludability for innovators and artists, which increases returns to valued works and innovations, and increases innovation.

Environmental entrepreneurs should pay special attention to the nature of property rights and the excludability of resources and or products because changes in the property rights system and the excludability of resources can create economic opportunities. Entrepreneurs who pursue opportunities related to property rights are termed *property rights entrepreneurs*. Property rights entrepreneurs establish excludability for open-access goods through the development and enforcement of property rights regimes. Property rights entrepreneurship can be accomplished in a number of ways.[15] *Political strategies* involve collaborating with government agencies to create new property rights regimes or to increase enforcement of existing ones. In one classic example, lighthouse keepers established excludability for their services by gaining the right to charge ships for lighthouse services at the local port.[16] Without the right to charge at port, lighthouse keepers would have had a difficult time excluding nonpayers from using the lighthouse. In Africa, elephant preservation has been aided by the assignment of herd ownership to local tribesmen.[17] In the western United States, the development of property rights regimes for water has helped, albeit imperfectly, allocate scarce water and encourage agricultural development. In fishing, producers have banded together to create transferable quota systems that allow a more sustainable harvest while preserving fishing rights.

The expansion of property rights can create opportunities beyond the environmental. For example, giving people real property rights through the enforcement of land titles can create game-changing opportunities in developing countries. As Hernando de Soto points out, many people in the developing world own assets, "but they lack the process to represent their property and create capital. They have houses but not titles, crops but not deeds, businesses but not statutes of incorporation."[18] The property rights entrepreneur seeks to alter the institutional environment such that property rights are defined and enforced, which allows for the development of opportunities within the system.

We can see how imperative a well-functioning property rights system is to the economic health of a society. In recent years there have been some interesting and groundbreaking developments in property rights regimes. A particularly interesting example of changes within property rights regimes is the idea of extended producer responsibility. *Extended producer responsibility,* or take-back, laws intend to reduce waste by altering property right systems. The basic idea is that producers are responsible for a product at the end of its useful life. In essence, ownership reverts to the producer after the useful life of the product. Because the producer must take back the product, it is expected that the price of the product will reflect its relative disposal costs, and producers will be motivated to reduce that cost in order to make their product more competitive. While not without their limitations, approaches that extend producer responsibility can provide advantage to entrepreneurial firms that figure out how to design their products for recycling, remanufacturing, disassembly, or lower cost handling and disposal.

As air pollution and the recognition of the potential for climate change has increased, it has become more obvious that air is a scarce and rivalrous good, and that property rights for air are important to the proper allocation of air resources, at least as a disposal mechanism for our waste. While most efforts to reduce pressure on air resources have been regulatory, a number of property rights regimes have also emerged. These have become popularly know as *cap-and-trade* regimes. The basic idea of a cap-and-trade regime is that property rights for air emissions are created, typically as an emissions permit. Each permit allows a certain level of emissions, and scarcity is created because only a limited number of permits are allowed. Permits are either distributed to existing firms, or sold by the government at auction. Once distributed, permits may be traded on the open market in order to encourage their allocation to the highest valued use.

Cap-and-trade systems were first used in the United States for the management of sulfur dioxide emissions in electricity generation, and they have been largely effective in reducing these emissions efficiently. A number of cap-and-trade regimes for carbon emissions exist worldwide. The foremost carbon cap-and-trade systems are operated under the Kyoto Protocol, signed by 191 countries. Cap-and-trade systems create commodities markets for emission permits and incent emission reductions because unused permits may be sold in these markets. Cap-and-trade regimes allow companies that can reduce emissions inexpensively to sell their rights to companies whose pollution control costs are higher. These systems also encourage technologies and processes that are less polluting because businesses with fewer emissions may sell, or do not need to purchase, emissions permits.

Technological strategies may also be used to enhance property rights regimes, establish excludability for a good, and create new opportunities.[19] The technique of branding cattle on the open range helped establish ownership and prevented the cattle from being stolen. The invention of barbed wire took that one step further and allowed landowners to keep their cattle on their land and cattle owned by others out. Technologies to prevent digital copying of music and videos enable excludability as well as artists' ability to choose whether or not they wish to freely share or sell their creations.

Motivating political action or developing technology to establish new property rights regimes is not a simple task. Political strategies often require collective action on the part of a group of entrepreneurs with shared interests in a particular outcome. Technological strategies require new thinking about how markets work and how enforcing new property rights can alter incentives. But perhaps most importantly, property rights regimes tend to evolve naturally as resources become scarce, and value can be captured in their preservation or efficient use. Understanding trends in property rights regimes for environmental and natural resources, and even contributing to their development, is a way for entrepreneurs to capture and create opportunities for more sustainable business models.

STRATEGY #2: INTERNALIZE EXTERNALITIES

In Chapter 2, we learned that the economic activity of one party can place costs (or benefits) on other parties. We referred to these costs (benefits) as externalities, and referred to them as side effects of one party's activity on another party for which no compensation is provided. These side effects can be positive or negative, and can be referred to as *external benefits* or *external costs*. That is, these effects may provide benefits to or incur costs on parties external to a transaction or economic activity. Externalities are also referred to as *spillover effects,* since they overflow onto parties not involved in the activity or exchange. The terms *positive externality* and *negative externality* are also used to indicate whether spillover effects are beneficial or detrimental to affected parties. The *institutional entrepreneur* develops new institutions that internalize externalities, and thereby enables more environmentally or socially sustainable ventures.[20]

Both positive and negative externalities are common in economic systems. Positive externalities, for example, may occur in the practice of beekeeping. While beekeepers traditionally keep bees for the harvesting of honey, bees also serve to pollinate orchards and crops. If the bees pollinate neighboring crops, the beekeeper is providing direct benefit to neighboring farms. Because it is difficult (or costly) to track such pollination services, it can difficult for beekeepers to get paid for pollination services. Positive externalities may also exist in real estate, especially in the case of retail stores. A large department store attracts customers, who may stop by a small eatery after shopping. Thus, the owner of the eatery next to such a store benefits from the increased traffic and commerce the department store creates. A similar dynamic occurs with golf courses and ski areas, where much of the benefit can accrue to holders of real estate surrounding golf courses or ski slopes.

One of the more interesting types of positive externalities is known as a *knowledge spillover,* which is often related to economic development. The term refers to knowledge, inventions, and technologies that cross organizational boundaries and benefit other companies than those that developed the knowledge. Knowledge spillovers occur through various means, but the movement of employees from one firm to another is a primary factor; such spillovers are one reason why technology ventures tend to cluster around universities and in regions like Silicon Valley.

In the previous chapter, we discussed how the burning of coal for electricity generation could create negative externalities because of emissions. Driving a gasoline-powered vehicle also releases emissions that, when combined with thousands of other vehicles, can create smog that has harmful health impacts. Scientists argue that the burning of fossil fuels, whether coal, oil, or natural gas, produces carbon emissions that create climate change and have associated impacts on ecosystems, land productivity, water supplies, and sea-level rise. Negative externalities also often arise in real estate. When an owner allows a property to fall into disrepair, it can substantially reduce the value of neighboring properties. A loud muffler or late-night party can impinge upon others' enjoyment of their environment, and runoff from pesticide and fertilizer use can impact fisheries and water quality downstream of agricultural lands.

Whether positive or negative, externalities can influence market outcomes, and institutional entrepreneurs are well aware of this. The inability to capture external benefits or to force others to pay their full external costs causes market perversions and can reduce entrepreneurial action in certain sectors. Most importantly, externalities can cause some entrepreneurial endeavors to be less financially attractive and others to be overly financially attractive. Firms producing substantive positive externalities are unable to capture as much value as they create. In short, it may be argued that organizations producing external benefits are underpaid for their products or services. In some instances, this means that the business is still viable; it is just not as competitive as it might be relative to alternatives. In other instances, the inability to appropriate the value created means the business is not at all viable. In contrast, firms creating substantive negative externalities are getting a bit of a free ride at the expense of others. In a market system, this makes them relatively more competitive.

Internalizing externalities refers to the process of eliminating externalities from market systems.[21] Entrepreneurs may gain from the internalization of either negative or positive externalities. When negative externalities exist, entrepreneurs in competing businesses or industries may figure out new ways of making individuals and organizations that create external costs pay those costs (forcing others to internalize their negative external costs). When positive externalities exist, entrepreneurs may figure out new ways to capture the value of the external benefits (in essence, preventing the dissipation of the benefits that the company creates).

Broadly speaking, internalizing externalities is achieved through the creation of new economic institutions, and the institutional entrepreneur is engaged in the process of developing new institutions that internalize externalities, whether positive or negative. The classic example, which we referred to earlier, is the patent system, which enables individuals and companies to benefit from their innovations. Many think that internalizing externalities requires government action. But entrepreneurs often find creative ways of capturing positive externalities or ensuring that competitors bear external costs.

Entrepreneurs can appropriate the value of positive externalities through innovative business models. Beekeepers, for example, eventually discovered that they could capture the value of pollination by transporting hives to farms in need of it. Because the hives can be moved on trucks, beekeepers are able to charge farms for pollination services while they benefit from the sale of honey produced.[22] The concept of a shopping mall may also be seen as a way to internalize the positive externalities of a retail location. The shopping mall rents to both the large "anchor stores" that attract customers and to the small eateries and specialty shops. Anchor stores typically pay less rent per square foot of space, effectively transferring some of the benefit created by the anchor store.[23] Golf courses are increasingly developed in concert with the surrounding residential lots, enabling the developer to capture the value created by the course for the surrounding real estate.

These methods may be referred to as *integration strategies* because they integrate different businesses in response to the externalities that may exist between them. When one business activity creates substantive positive externalities for another, integration strategies can be used to increase profitability of the business creating those benefits, by buying, or developing, both businesses at the same time. Another example of a positive externality can be farming mussels in nutrient rich waters. Seawater that is overly dense in nutrients can cause fish to suffocate, which is a major environmental concern. Mussel farming in nutrient dense water has been shown to be a viable way to reduce excess nutrients in coastal water while producing a high-value seafood product at the same time.[24]

Entrepreneurs can also benefit by forcing competitors to internalize negative externalities. This may be achieved in a variety of ways. One way is through the development of taxes that require producers to pay a sum equivalent to the negative externalities they produce. These are referred to as *Pigouvian taxes,* named after the economist, Arthur Pigou, who first suggested taxes as a means of alleviating market effects of negative externalities. Theoretically, a Pigouvian tax forces polluters to internalize the costs of production, which raises prices for products that are harmful to the environment.[25] In such case, products that produce environmental damages will be more expensive for customers and be at a cost or price disadvantage relative to similar products that cause less harm. A Pigouvian tax, therefore, is designed to enable full-cost pricing. Note that this is not a tax used to repair environmental degradation, but rather one that internalizes the cost of the damage in the price of the good. Pigouvian taxes benefit entrepreneurs in industries with competing products that can be produced without similar harmful effects, and therefore with less tax.

Gasoline taxes are a type of Pigouvian tax because they force consumers to internalize some of the external costs of fuel use (such as the creation of smog).

Carbon taxes (taxes levied on carbon emissions of various sorts) are another (and related) type of Pigouvian tax. Both could make entrepreneurial activity in renewable energy industries more attractive because the higher cost of fossil fuels makes renewable energy options more competitive in the marketplace.

While Pigouvian taxes may be useful for solving many externality problems, they are far from a perfect solution. There are three main challenges posed by Pigouvian taxes. The first is the challenge of calculating the correct level of tax to apply. It is hard to agree on what level of pollution one is willing to accept in relation to the price one is willing to pay for the good. If the tax is too high, then society's demand is not being met, and people's utility is not being maximized. On the other hand, if the tax is too low, then society will demand more of the good and too much pollution will occur, making society as a whole worse off. The second challenge to Pigouvian taxes is that they are subject to political manipulation, which may cause them to be set at a less than ideal level (the level that is equivalent to the external damages). The last challenge is that they have generally proven to be difficult to create because they have been politically unpopular in many countries, particularly in the United States. They nevertheless remain as a tool, or at the least a source of opportunity, for environmental entrepreneurs wishing to level the playing field for environmentally superior products and services.

Regulatory strategies may also be utilized to force producers of negative externalities to internalize costs. Often referred to as *command and control,* regulation requires producers to follow specific guidelines of behavior in the production process. *Performance standards* typically require producers of pollution to limit emissions to a certain level. *Prescriptive standards* require the utilization of specific technologies or processes for pollution abatement. Both performance and prescriptive standards are in popular use throughout the world to control emissions into air, water, and soil. As with taxes, such regulations can aid environmental entrepreneurs by limiting the negative externalities created by competing producers. Dupont, for example, was argued to have benefited from the ban on chlorofluorocarbons (used as refrigerants), which depleted the ozone layer in the upper atmosphere. Scientists realized that commonly used chlorofluorocarbons were destroying the ozone layer and allowing cancer-causing radiation to reach the earth's surface. After analyzing the scientific data, Dupont came out in support of the ban and committed to ceasing the production of chlorofluorocarbons. In the 1980s, politicians in developed countries agreed to the Montreal Protocol, which banned the production of the primary ozone-depleting chemicals. Dupont, had taken a bold stance, but also had developed chemical alternatives, which it then offered to the marketplace.

Voluntary industry initiatives may also be useful, particularly among firms with superior environmental technologies or products. Such initiatives often take the form of standard setting, wherein stakeholders agree on certain rules of behavior and producers decide whether they wish to follow those standards. Those who do may benefit from the ability to market their compliance to their customer base. The Forest Stewardship Council (FSC), for example, certifies lumber to ten principles of responsible forest management. The Home Depot, a retailer of hardware and lumber products now carries FSC certified lumber. The International Organization for Standardization (ISO) 14000 environmental management standards provides another example of stakeholder generated standards. The ISO 14000 standards are management standards that prescribe systems for governing the environmental aspects of an organization's operations. A facility or company can be certified to the ISO 14000 standards and use that certification to communicate to external stakeholders that they are managing their environmental performance.

One of the best ways to internalize externalities is through property rights strategies, which we discussed in the prior section.[26] Indeed, many economists suggest that all externality problems are, in essence, property rights problems. But externalities may also be understood as a transaction cost problem. *Transactions costs* refer to the costs of exchange as opposed to the cost of production and include the costs of searching for information on products, negotiation, contracting, and enforcement of contracts. Where transaction costs are higher than the value of an exchange, it is possible that the exchange is not completed, leading to a suboptimal economic outcome and an opportunity left on the table. If indeed the goal of the transaction is to make both parties better off, then both parties lose an opportunity to increase their well-being. For the institutional entrepreneur, strategies to reduce transaction costs are perhaps the most effective in correcting for market failures and creating an opportunity for a sustainable venture.

Technology also plays a major role in lowering the cost of gathering information. Moreover, understanding the institutional environment in which one is participating is equally imperative, especially in the pursuit of sustainable venture opportunities. This is because the legal and regulatory environment can differ from country to country. Having the ability to enforce contracts and other legally binding agreements will allow parties to more swiftly come to terms. If negotiations and contract enforcement take too long or are uncertain, the agreement may be tough to finalize. Institutional entrepreneurs try to build certainty into their agreements and tend to operate in legal environments that afford them retribution if the other party does not uphold their end of the bargain.

As we can see, there are multiple opportunities for institutional entrepreneurs to exploit if they know where to look. By internalizing externalities through regulatory strategies, voluntary industry initiatives or by lowering transaction costs, entrepreneurs can develop and act upon entrepreneurial opportunities, which results in the possibility of generating profit while providing societal or environmental value.

STRATEGY #3: DEVELOP INFORMATIONAL STRUCTURES

The *informational entrepreneur* develops new market information systems that provide traction in markets and make them more efficient. Informational entrepreneurs have been prevalent in the market for environmentally oriented products and services. Indeed, informational entrepreneurs have been active in markets as diverse as organic foods, green buildings, renewable energy, energy efficiency, and sustainable forestry. The key to the success of these programs has been in creating systems that provide valid information to customers regarding the green or social attributes of a product or service. These informational entrepreneurs have resolved the common difficulty customers have had telling whether a product or service was actually more environmentally or socially friendly than other products.[27]

Business strategists refer to this problem as *information asymmetry*.[28] Information asymmetry typically refers to the fact that sellers of products have access to superior information about the product or service than do buyers—that is, the available information is asymmetrical because one side has more of it than the other. Information asymmetry can diminish the efficiency of markets or even result in the failure of a market to exist at all.

Information asymmetry has been historically prevalent in markets for green products and services. The green building market is a good case in point. Not very long ago, it was very difficult for customers interested in the benefits of green buildings to distinguish between buildings that were truly green, and those that were not. This occurs because it is relatively easy for a builder to claim a building is green, when it is actually not, which creates a competitive dynamic in which those who are not authentic green builders have a cost advantage over those who are authentic.

In the United States, a certification system for green buildings, known as Leadership in Energy and Environmental Design (LEED), was implemented to solve the information problem. Created by the U.S. Green Building Council, the LEED program certifies new and existing buildings according to a set of efficiency, environmental, materials, and other criteria. Third parties certify buildings to help assure customers that the building meets LEED criteria. The system has helped provide traction to the market for green buildings and has spawned an industry of architects, consultants, builders, and other entrepreneurs looking to build more efficient and effective buildings.

Similar third-party certification and labeling systems for environmental products and services have had similar effects. Common examples include certification systems for energy efficiency in appliances (Energy Star), organic foods (U.S. Organic Foods Production Act), renewable energy credits (Green-e), fair trade (fair-trade coffee), and sustainable forestry (Forest Stewardship Council). While some of these are supported or sponsored by governments (i.e., the organic foods labeling system and Energy Star program), many have emerged as nonprofit organizations that support industry participants and others who share the goal of differentiating their products to customers. Most programs are associated with a label that may be attached to products that meet the certification standards, which is a way to communicate the product's attributes to the customer. Most certifications are also performed by a third party (not by the producer of the product) to help insure that the certification is authentic. After all, the credibility and success of these systems is dependent upon the validity of the criteria and the trustworthiness of their certification process. Debates of the nature of the specific criteria often follow, and systems to monitor the authenticity of certification are critical.

Regardless, certification and labeling systems for products with environmental or social aspects can help make markets for them work more effectively. By providing a means of communicating environmental and social benefits to consumers, they solve information asymmetry problems and help customers benefit from environmentally superior offerings. Most important, the emergence or creation of new, trustworthy certification and labeling systems represent an opportunity for environmental entrepreneurs to profit from the benefits they create.

Strong brands can have a similar informational effect, providing customers with some assurance that the companies' products or services meet expectations for superior environmental or social performance. Patagonia, for example, has built a brand that many customers affiliate with superior environmental performance not only by creating top-performing products with an "ironclad guarantee" for customer satisfaction, but also by making sure that their products are manufactured in the most environmentally and socially responsible manner. They are transparent in the facilities that they use in their global production, and they employ third-party auditors to ensure that their suppliers adhere to Patagonia's Social and Environmental Responsibility Guidelines. They also report their environmental stewardship measures on their webpage called the "Footprint Chronicles," which documents some of the environmental and social impacts of key products from design through shipping.[29]

To the degree that customers care about the social or environmental attributes of their purchases, businesses can benefit by signaling their superior attributes through branding and certification programs, achieving potential competitive advantage in the marketplace. In Chapter 5, we will further address the nature of markets for social and environmental attributes, and discuss the means by which companies can successfully market those attributes.

STRATEGY #4: TRANSFORM GOVERNMENT INTERVENTION

Government intervention in markets is pervasive throughout the world. Intervention takes a variety of forms, including taxes, subsidies, and regulations. Whether one sees such intervention as a good or bad activity, the reality is that such intervention affects the competitive dynamics of markets. All too often, such intervention benefits entrenched interests with the power to influence political decisions. It may also benefit relatively dirty or harmful activities that are not in the best interest of society or ecological sustainability. Increasingly, however, governments are altering their perspective and providing greater support for environmental entrepreneurs. Motivating, or even just understanding, the nature of these changes can be a source of substantial opportunity for aspiring environmental entrepreneurs.

Political entrepreneurs motivate changes to taxes, subsidies or other government incentive structures to increase the competitive position of their companies and enable a more profitable venture.[30] Political entrepreneurship may be used by sustainable entrepreneurs to enhance the viability of a more social or environmentally sustainable venture. Political strategies can be quite effective for environmental entrepreneurs because the wind of popular opinion or ecological virtue may be at their back. In many cases, this support has allowed environmental entrepreneurs and associated stakeholders to emerge victorious over powerful and entrenched political interests. Often, the ability to revolutionize the nature of government intervention rests in the need to eliminate negative externalities, or more broadly speaking, to solve a social or environmental problem. It usually involves partnerships with stakeholders who have shared goals, which can create unusual, but sometimes productive, alliances.

Political changes and strategies have created substantive opportunities for renewable energy companies throughout the world. In Germany, the renewable energy sector has been buoyed by generous feed-in tariffs, which offer higher rates to generators using renewable technologies. In Japan, subsidies and a broad effort to decrease the island nation's reliance on imported energy helped make Sharp, Kyocera, and Sanyo some of the leading producers of solar cells. China has also recently been a supporter of renewable energy, and its companies now hold significant market share in solar cell production.

While these governments' decisions may be motivated by economic development and monetary gain, the result is a system that is friendlier to environmentally sustainable products and services. Regardless of the intent of the government, the political entrepreneur must be able to recognize the social or environmental impacts of all types of legal and regulatory decisions, as there may exist an opportunity to exploit the dynamic political system. In the United States, numerous states have passed renewable portfolio standards that require electricity producers to generate a certain percentage of their power from renewable sources. As of 2011, twenty-nine states had passed renewable portfolio standards, and the laws have spawned an industry of solar power installers in many of those states. U.S. policy has also strongly supported the biofuels industry, which created a boom in corn-based ethanol production, as well as significant investment into technology development for cellulosic ethanol and other biofuels. Most recently, the U.S. government has been stimulating the development of electric vehicle and associated battery technologies.

Efforts to alter the competitive position of environmental entrepreneurs may take a variety of forms, including taxation policy, regulatory policy, or more direct subsidies. Taxation policy can include tax credits or deductions for certain activities (often capital investments), or direct taxes. In the United States, the renewable energy production tax credit allowed those who install renewable generation capacity a tax credit of 2.2-cents/kilowatt hour of energy produced, for the first ten years of a facility's operation. The tax credit had a substantial impact on the installation of wind-power generation in the United States. Other tax credit programs support home insulation contractors, energy-efficient appliance manufacturers, and electric vehicle producers. As discussed earlier, direct taxes may also penalize polluting industries, which can benefit businesses with cleaner technologies or products.

We would be remiss if we did not address a few caveats. Altering the nature of government intervention is no easy task. Success depends on the complex dynamics of public attitudes and political decision-making. In addition, promoting government intervention can create a number of unanticipated problems, both philosophical and practical. At a philosophical level, government intervention is often seen as counter to the functioning of a healthy free-market economy. Indeed, placing decision-making authority for the success of an industry in the hands of politicians can result in poor investments. A case in point may be the various policies that created the boom in corn-based ethanol production in the United States. While the policies were clearly successful in generating entrepreneurial action, many argue that the energy expended to produce these fuels is almost as great as the energy they are purported to conserve. In other cases, such as the renewable energy production tax credit, changes in the credit over time have created boom/bust cycles in the installation of wind turbines.

Yet, within the space of global competition, nations often find themselves competing against countries where substantive national investments in certain industries are made. The term *industrial policy* describes the extent and direction of government investment and support in certain industries or sectors. In some countries, such as Japan and Germany (and more recently the United States and China), industrial policy has strongly supported investment in industries such as renewable energy. Such subsidies can be utilized to help generate jobs and new ventures in important new areas, and it may be difficult to compete without them.

Unfortunately, government policy may also be utilized as a tool to redistribute wealth to certain sectors or individuals. *Rent-seeking* refers to efforts to manipulate the political process for individual or organizational gain without an associated benefit to the social good or the functioning of free markets.[31] It is often difficult to untangle rent-seeking efforts from efforts to generate support for new and important industries that are in society's best interest. The goal of the environmental entrepreneur is to navigate these difficult issues to create sensible support for industries and sectors that have better ecological outcomes, but make economic sense. Typically, this means garnering support for industries that produce fewer negative externalities or generate greater positive ones. At the least, it seems that leveling the playing field by eliminating government subsidies for ecologically damaging activities should be a top priority of the environmental or political entrepreneur.

STRATEGY #5: BREAK MONOPOLY POWER

The *market-appropriating entrepreneur* breaks the monopoly power (or more generally market power) of incumbent firms in an industry.[32] A *monopoly* means that there is only one supplier of a particular good or service. *Oligopoly* means that there are only a few suppliers of a particular product or service. In either case, competition may be reduced, and consumers can encounter higher prices from the lack of competition. Economists argue that monopolists are able to price their products above the competitive price and thereby achieve higher profits. Industries characterized by monopoly represent opportunities for entrepreneurs because of the potential to capture some of the excess profits within the industry. Entrepreneurs can appropriate some of the profit by eating into the monopoly power of an incumbent.

Natural monopolies exist when economies of scale are so large that there can be only one efficient producer of the product or service. In short, it is less expensive for one firm to produce all of the output required by the market. For many years, it was argued that electricity production and long-distance communications were natural monopolies and that the most efficient means of production was a single firm. Often, such industries are regulated in an attempt to insure that prices remain at a competitive level. Regulation may also result in a *statutory monopoly,* in which the status of the monopoly is assured by government policy. This is often the case with electrical power utilities subject to a regulatory authority that controls electricity prices so that the monopolist has the only legal right to serve a given geographical market. Some monopolies also exist as government-owned entities in which the state retains control over the providers' decisions.

Many argue that industries characterized by monopoly, oligopoly, or market power more generally tend to become technologically stagnant and shun the introduction of new technologies. This may be the result of the removal of competition, in which case companies lack the incentive to introduce new ideas or methods. Thus, another way to generate opportunity for environmentally friendly businesses is by breaking the monopoly power of stagnant industries. Because monopolistic industries have a tendency to not innovate, the persistence of monopoly power often dissuades technological advancement that is more environmentally friendly. In addition, monopolistic industries are an attractive target because they are often highly profitable.

Breaking monopoly power is, of course, difficult, because monopolists are often highly entrenched in their industries and are interested in defending their positions. But it may be accomplished in a number of ways. In the case of natural monopolies, the answer usually lies in technologies that operate efficiently at smaller scale. Nucor Steel and other "mini-mills," for example, successfully competed against large integrated steel manufacturers by using innovative techniques for recycling steel into high-grade steel products. In the case of statutory monopolies, alternative providers need to make the case to politicians and legal authorities that they can successfully compete within an industry. MCI, an innovative telecommunications company, successfully made the case to authorities that the statutory monopoly over long-distance telecommunications in the United States was unjustified. The result was the break up of AT&T into a group of regional telecommunications providers and long-distance services. Their case was made more robust by the advent of microwave-based relay station technology, which eliminated the necessity of carrying signals over copper wires.

In the electricity generation industry, a number of developments have helped eliminate the strong monopoly power of utilities and increased opportunities for environmental entrepreneurs. The first has been the advent of technologies that allow electricity to be produced on a small scale at reasonable cost. *Distributed generation* refers to electricity production that occurs at small scale at or near its point of use. Distributed generation benefits from the fact that electricity does not have to be transmitted across large distances, but it typically results in higher costs of production compared to those of large centralized generating facilities. Distributed generation technologies include solar and wind power, as well as natural gas turbines.

The second development has been the advent of various regulatory changes that have forced utilities to accept electricity generated by other sources. Most U.S. states, for example, require utilities to accommodate customers who generate their own electricity. This is accomplished through *net metering* policies which allow customers with solar power or other electricity generation capacity to provide that capacity to the electrical grid when they are producing more than they use. Their electrical meter records the power provided to the grid and subtracts the amount from the total amount they use. The electricity customers only pay for the difference between what they use and what they produce. In other words, the landscape of power generation can be transformed from one large monopoly to many distributed sites that actually produce power for public consumption. Net metering laws have enabled electricity customers to install solar and wind generation and to benefit from their production when it exceeds their use. The laws have helped encourage new ventures in solar power system installation. A number of states have also deregulated their electricity utility industries, and customers can now choose their power providers. Some of these providers, such as Green Mountain Energy, offer renewable energy options to customers in deregulated states.

Key Learnings

In this chapter we discussed how an entrepreneur could help create opportunities for sustainable ventures. We drew upon the idea of exploiting market failures to develop institutional contexts that allow entrepreneurs to create new economic opportunities.

The first strategy for creating opportunity from a market failure is to define and enforce property rights. A property rights entrepreneur implements new means of defining or enforcing property rights in order to enable a profitable venture. Recall what happens when there are no property rights assigned to a good. The tragedy of the commons is a powerful example of what can happen when a group has unlimited access to use a good, but individual's are not responsible for its maintenance or the effects of their actions. Property rights entrepreneurs establish excludability for public and common goods through the development and enforcement of property rights regimes. Some political strategies involve collaborating with government agencies to create new property rights regimes or increase enforcement of existing ones. Cap-and-trade is an example of creating and enforcing property rights.

Technological strategies are also used to enhance property rights regimes, establish excludability for a good, and create new opportunities. Technological strategies may be easier to implement than political strategies, which may require a coordinated group effort. Technological strategies require new thinking about how markets work and how enforcing new property rights can alter incentives in the market. A rudimentary example of a technological innovation is the use of branding to identify one's cattle on the open range and the use of barbed wire to delineate private property and to keep one's own livestock in and another's out.

The second strategy we have investigated is the internalization of externalities. Externalities are the side effects of one party's activity on another party for which no compensation is provided, and they can be either positive or negative. The institutional entrepreneur develops new institutions that internalize externalities, making the producers of external costs pay for those costs, or enabling those who produce external benefits to capture those benefits. Internalizing externalities may allow more environmentally or socially sustainable ventures. Generally, the internalization of externalities is achieved through the creation of new economic institutions. While this may require government intervention in some instances, clever entrepreneurs find innovative ways to appropriate the value of positive externalities through creative business models. Entrepreneurs can also benefit by forcing competitors to internalize negative externalities. We have discussed one way to do this through the creation of Pigouvian taxes, which are taxes that require the producers to pay a sum equivalent to the negative externalities they produce. Regulatory strategies and voluntary industry initiatives are other approaches an entrepreneur can use to create opportunities via the internalization of externalities.

The third strategy we have explored is the development of informational structures—a strategy employed by the informational entrepreneur, who seeks to rectify information asymmetry and develops new market information systems that provide traction in markets to make them more efficient. We see informational entrepreneurs most often in the market for environmentally oriented products and services, like organic foods, green buildings, renewable energy, energy efficiency, and sustainable forestry. The key to the success of these programs has been creating systems that provide valid information to customers regarding the green attributes of a product or service. Examples of successful development of informational structures include the certified organic food program and the LEED certified building program.

The fourth strategy that entrepreneurs can use to create opportunity for a sustainable venture is to transform government intervention. Government intervention in markets is pervasive throughout the world and can include taxes, subsidies, and regulations; it also skews the free market, and all too often, such intervention benefits entrenched interests with the power to influence political decisions. Political entrepreneurs motivate changes to taxes subsidies or other government incentive structures to make their individual or corporate position more competitive. Political entrepreneurship is a strategy that environmental entrepreneurs may use to bolster the viability of their social or environmentally sustainable venture.

The fifth and final strategy an entrepreneur can use to create opportunities by exploiting market failures is to break monopoly power. We call this approach to entrepreneurship *market-appropriating entrepreneurship.* A monopoly is the condition in which there is a sole supplier of a good or service; in the presence of a monopoly, many would argue, technological innovation becomes stagnant. One way for a market-appropriating entrepreneur to break monopoly power is to introduce game-changing technology and disruptive innovations that operate more effectively and efficiently at a smaller scale. Although this is indeed challenging, the rewards for an entrepreneur that innovates a strategy to break monopoly power can be substantial.

The bottom line is that for an entrepreneur who identifies market failures or suboptimally performing markets, specific strategies can be employed to create value and generate rewards within the economic system. In some cases this requires recognizing emerging changes in the system. In other instances this requires changing the system itself.

Endnotes

1. D. F. Pacheco, T. J. Dean, and D. Payne, "Escaping the Green Prison: Entrepreneurship and the Creation of Opportunities for Sustainable Development," *Journal of Business Venturing* 25, no. 5 (2010): 464–480.
2. T. J. Dean and J. McMullen, "Toward a Theory of Sustainable Entrepreneurship: Reducing Environmental Degradation through Entrepreneurial Action," *Journal of Business Venturing* 22, no. 1 (2007): 50–76.
3. T. L. Andersen and Peter J. Hill, *The Not So Wild, Wild, West: Property Rights on the New Frontier* (Stanford, CA: Stanford University Press, 2004).
4. Dean and McMullen, "Toward a Theory of Sustainable Entrepreneurship: Reducing Environmental Degradation through Entrepreneurial Action."
5. E. G. Furubotn and S. Pejovich, "Property Rights and Economic Theory: A Survey of Recent Literature," *Journal of Economic Literature* 10, no. 4 (1972), 1137–1162.
6. A. A. Alchian and H. Demsetz, "The Property Rights Paradigm," *Journal of Economic History* 33, no. 1 (1973): 16–27.
7. T. Eggertson, *Economic Behavior and Institutions* (Cambridge: Cambridge University Press, 1990).
8. Furubotn and S. Pejovich, "Property Rights and Economic Theory: A Survey of Recent Literature."
9. Eggertson, *Economic Behavior and Institutions*
10. Ibid.
11. D. H. Cole, "New forms of private property: property rights on environmental goods," in *Encyclopedia of Law and Economics,* ed. B. Bouckaert and G. Geest, 274–314 (Northampton, MA: Edward Elgar, 2000).
12. Ibid.
13. G. Hardin, "The Tragedy of the Commons," *Journal of Science* 162 (1968):1243–1248.
14. A. Randall, "The Problem of Market Failure," in *Economics of the Environment: Selected Readings,* ed. R. Dorfman and N. S. Dorfman (New York: W.W. Norton, 1993): 144–161.
15. Dean and McMullen, "Toward a Theory of Sustainable Entrepreneurship: Reducing Environmental Degradation through Entrepreneurial Action."

16. R. H. Coase, "The Lighthouse in Economics," *Journal of Law and Economics* 17 (October 1974): 357–376.
17. T. L. Anderson and D. Leal *Enviro-Capitalists: Doing Good while Doing Well* (Lanham, MD: Rowman and Littlefield, 1997).
18. H. DeSoto, "The Mystery of Capital," *Finance and Development* 38, no. 1 (2000): 29–34, 7.
19. Furubotn and S. Pejovich, "Property Rights and Economic Theory: A Survey of Recent Literature."
20. Dean and McMullen, "Toward a Theory of Sustainable Entrepreneurship: Reducing Environmental Degradation through Entrepreneurial Action."
21. H. Demsetz, "Toward a Theory of Property Rights," *American Economic Review* 57, no. 2(1967), 347–359.
22. S. N. S. Cheung, "The Fable of the Bees: An Economic Investigation," *Journal of Law and Economics* 16, no. 1(1973): 11–33
23. B. P. Pashigian and E. D. Gould, "Internalizing Externalities: The Pricing of Space in Shopping Malls" *Journal of Law and Economics* 41, no. 1 (1998): 115–142.
24. I. M. Gren, O. Lindahl, and M. Lindqvist, "Values of Mussel Farming for Combating Eutrophication: An Application to the Baltic Sea," *Ecological Engineering* 35 (2009):935–945.
25. A. C. Pigou, *The Economics of Welfare*, 4th ed. (London: Macmillan, 1932).
26. Demsetz, H., 1967. Toward a theory of property rights. American Economic Review 57, no. 2 (1967): 347–359.
27. Dean and McMullen, "Toward a Theory of Sustainable Entrepreneurship: Reducing Environmental Degradation through Entrepreneurial Action."
28. G. A. Akerlof, G.A., "The Market for Lemons: Quality Uncertainty and the Market Mechanism," *Quarterly Journal of Economics* 84 (1970): 488–500.
29. "Environmentalism," Patagonia website, at http://www.patagonia.com/environmentalism, retrieved January 21, 2012.
30. Dean and McMullen, "Toward a Theory of Sustainable Entrepreneurship: Reducing Environmental Degradation through Entrepreneurial Action."
31. Anne O. Krueguer, "The Political Economy of the Rent-Seeking Society," *American Economic Review* 64, no. 3 (June 1974): 291–303.
32. Dean and McMullen, "Toward a Theory of Sustainable Entrepreneurship: Reducing Environmental Degradation through Entrepreneurial Action."

SOCIAL ENTREPRENEURSHIP

INTRODUCTION

Although individuals, organizations, and governments have actively combated the ills that afflict our societies, many observers believe that progress remains unsatisfactory on several fronts. After all, we continue to live in a world troubled by poverty, hunger, disease, social injustice, and armed conflict. While many of these problems appear unsolvable, global entrepreneurial and political communities are espousing a new way of thinking about solutions to our most intractable social problems. That new way of thinking is called *social entrepreneurship*. Social entrepreneurship embraces a combination of enterprise management skills, innovative products and services, and new business models that offer the opportunity to solve social challenges through entrepreneurial initiative and market and extra-market incentives. Social entrepreneurs share an underlying ethos, which is focused on applying entrepreneurial ideas, concepts, and methods to make positive social change in the world.

The term *social entrepreneurship* has emerged as a way to conceptualize this ethos and point to entrepreneurship as a means of resolving social ills. As an emerging concept and real world phenomenon, social entrepreneurship has attracted the attention of politicians, executives, activists, philanthropists, and even investors. It is, indeed, a global trend of increasing importance and hope. Most important, a wide variety of innovative social entrepreneurs are creating new business and nonprofit models that are helping to build communities, enable the poor, and deliver solutions to challenges such as malnutrition, disease, poverty, and injustice. As with traditional entrepreneurship, many people are drawn to the idea of social entrepreneurship because it is exciting to witness an enterprise fight against the odds to implement an extraordinary idea with lasting impact. In many cases, the odds facing social entrepreneurs are tremendously high, as they are combating challenges the world has faced for decades, centuries, or even millennia.

For purposes of this book we view social entrepreneurship as a subset of the broader concepts of sustainable venturing and traditional entrepreneurship. We define *social entrepreneurship* as the process of creating social value by bringing together a unique combination of resources to pursue an opportunity. *Social entrepreneurship is distinguished by the entrepreneur's mission to create social value, and the prioritization of social value creation over the generation of personal or organizational financial wealth.* Gregory Dees, one of the concept's early proponents, proposes the social entrepreneur as "one species in the genus entrepreneur," those "with a social mission."[1] Social entrepreneurs prioritize doing good (for society) over doing well (financially). Personally, they may sacrifice income for the intrinsic satisfaction of achieving social benefit. Organizationally, social ventures may experience less than competitive returns, making them less profitable or perhaps dependent upon charitable donations or government support. In other cases, innovative social entrepreneurs find the means of creating sufficient revenue to enable the continuation, scalability, and profitability of their ventures. Ideally, they achieve rates of return that are competitive with other ventures and thereby attract more entrepreneurs and investors into their efforts.

Social entrepreneurs often fill the voids left by inadequate government budgets and capabilities, or subpar economic incentive systems. Opportunities abound in both urban and rural settings, and in both developing and developed country contexts. The scope of social ventures can vary from large-scale microfinance operations in Bangladesh to small-scale community gardens in New York City. They increasingly span the range from innovative nonprofits to exciting new hybrid business models to social-value driven for-profit enterprises.

In addition, the persistence and range of some social problems is so vast that many see an enormous opportunity to employ entrepreneurial methods for the social good. With the advent of the twenty-first century, the United Nations (in concert with other international organizations) released a set of international development goals called the "Millenium Development Goals." The goals are focused on social challenges familiar to many, including (1) eradicating extreme poverty and hunger, (2) achieving universal primary education, (3) promoting gender equality and empowering women, (4) reducing child mortality, (5) improving maternal health, and (6) combating HIV/AIDS, malaria and other diseases.[2] The UN Millennium Development Goals point to the most critical social challenges facing global populations and serve as a manifesto of opportunity for entrepreneurial action.

Adding to the legitimacy of the field of social entrepreneurship are the many support organizations that are pouring capital into the field as a catalyst for change. Two examples of such organizations are the Ashoka Foundation and the Acumen Fund. Ashoka's mission is to "shape a global, entrepreneurial, competitive citizen sector: one that allows social entrepreneurs to thrive and enables the world's citizens to think and act as change makers."[3] The organization has a three-tiered approach to their mission:

1. Support social entrepreneurs through investment and guidance.
2. Promote group entrepreneurship through global networks of change agents.
3. Build infrastructure in the field by working with investors, academic institutions, financing entities, and by fostering partnerships that deliver social value.[4]

Like the Ashoka Foundation, the Acumen Fund believes in using entrepreneurship as a means to addressing the world's problems, primarily through investments in early-stage enterprises and by focusing on what it calls *patient capital.* The goal of patient capital is to maximize impact over long time horizons rather than immediate financial return. Acumen's investments are risk-tolerant, flexible with public/private partnerships, and support the entrepreneur with management tools.[5] Other organizations that support enterprises in the social sector are the Bill and Melinda Gates Foundation and the Clinton Global Initiative.

Social entrepreneurship is increasingly viewed as a solution to many of these challenges. At the most basic level, many see the encouragement of entrepreneurial activity as a means of improving the conditions and quality of life of impoverished nations and communities. For various reasons, the benefits of markets and entrepreneurial innovation have yet to reach large sectors of the global population.

The increasing focus on entrepreneurship as the solution is also a response to many failed, or at least disappointing, attempts to solve social problems through charity or large-scale international development projects. At the highest level, social entrepreneurs are implementing enterprises with products and services that have direct benefit to the poor or others in need. Indeed, social entrepreneurship is increasingly viewed as the platform to deliver innovative sources of energy, more healthful and efficient biomass cookstoves, water pumps, and other products and services.

TYPES OF SOCIAL VENTURES

Social ventures may vary from exclusively nonprofit organizations to for-profit social business ventures.[6] *Nonprofit social ventures* utilize innovation and business methods to increase efficiency and provide superior value through nonprofit organizational structures. Though they often are unable to garner sufficient market revenues to cover costs, they embrace entrepreneurial innovation and leverage the resources that are available to them. *Hybrid, nonprofit social ventures* combine revenue-generating activities with nonprofit structures to deliver social value. At the most basic level, such nonprofit organizations operate side businesses that provide a stream of income for their activities. The Salvation Army, for example, operates thrift stores using volunteers to support a host of social activities. Many small nonprofits, such as fire departments and ambulance corps, sell baked goods, sandwiches, or other products and services to raise funds. Increasingly, however, nonprofits are discovering innovative means of generating income from the services they provide, even if that income does not completely cover their costs. Their funding is an innovative combination of revenue-generating activities and charitable or government contributions. In this way, charitable organizations are able to leverage their donations for greatest impact.

In addition, many nonprofits leverage revenues through unique enterprise models and financial structures. Habitat for Humanity, for example, uses an innovative model to build and rehabilitate homes for families in need, engaging volunteers in construction and seeking donations for building materials. Habitat for Humanity also requires families to work on the construction of their own homes. Down payments and mortgages are utilized to build the home. To date, Habitat for Humanity has built over a half-million affordable houses and has affiliates throughout the world.[7]

Another model is to operate research, product design, and manufacturing as a nonprofit organization, but to distribute the final product sales through for-profit channels. Envirofit International, for example, operates as a nonprofit organization focused on the design and manufacture of efficient biomass cook stoves for developing countries. The company works with for-profit dealerships throughout Africa and Asia and has sold over 300,000 stoves that decrease biomass consumption and helps reduce indoor air pollution. IDE Technologies takes a similar approach in marketing foot-treadle water pumps and other manual irrigation technologies. Its pumps allow greater use of irrigation and increase income for farmers as well as entrepreneurs in developing countries. Such hybrid nonprofit social ventures have found ways to combine the good intentions of founders and donors with market-driven action.

Social business ventures operate as for-profits, but prioritize their social missions over financial returns. They epitomize a new generation of social entrepreneurs who combine a passion for change with an understanding of the importance of market incentives. Tom's Shoes, for example, operates as a for-profit enterprise with a strong social mission. For every pair of shoes purchased from Tom's Shoes, its nonprofit affiliate donates a pair to a child in need. Its stylish but simple shoes, combined with their "one for one" donation model, has proven successful in attracting customers. To date, Tom's Shoes has given away more than one million shoes throughout the world, helping children in impoverished regions avoid cuts, infection, and soil-born diseases.[8]

Often, the business models of social business ventures are more scalable because they can take on equity capital, provide some level of returns to investors, and embrace market-driven business models. They often seek a new class of investors who are interested in both financial and social returns. Such investors find social business ventures increasingly attractive because they combine the discipline of markets with the potential for transformational social and environmental impacts. More details regarding the growing landscape of funding opportunities for social and sustainable ventures can be found in Chapter 7, "Financing the Sustainable Venture."

Social business ventures may sacrifice some level of profitability to achieve their social goals. This can create conflict, particularly in public companies, which are legally bound to maximize shareholder financial wealth. In the most famous example, the board of Ben & Jerry's Ice Cream was compelled to sell the company to Unilever at least partially because it was required by law to maximize shareholder value. In response to this conflict, new legal forms of organization are arising to accommodate social founders and investors. The *low-profit limited-liability* (L3C) legal structure is now available in a number of states in the United States. Like a Limited Liability Corporation, the L3C limits investor liability and offers pass-through taxation, but enables the enterprise to prioritize social goals over financial ones. The *benefit corporation* is another new corporate legal structure that requires the organization to operate to the *public benefit,* defined as a material positive benefit to society and the environment. Benefit corporations must have a social or environmental intent and serve the interests of workers, the environment, and community, as well as shareholders. Outdoor clothing company Patagonia was the first company to become a registered benefit corporation in California. The United Kingdom also allows the formation of *community interest companies,* which permit the pursuit of similar missions. Whether these new organizational forms will prove successful remains to be seen, but they are gaining in popularity. At the least, they open up new options for social and environmental entrepreneurs (and their investors) who wish to prioritize social or environmental benefit.[9, 10]

Whether they operate legally as for-profit, nonprofit, or hybrid organizations, social ventures may also be conceptualized according to the nature of the market conditions that exist for their enterprise activities. Social ventures may thus be categorized as *market-driven, market-augmented, extra-market,* or *market-convergent. Market-driven social enterprises* are those that are financially viable under current market conditions. In other words, such enterprises garner sufficient revenues from the sales of their products and services to cover their costs of operation and enable their survival in competitive markets, while achieving their social missions. In many ways, such organizations look like any other venture. Yet they prioritize their social missions in their decisions and actions. An example of a market-driven social enterprise is Green Mountain Coffee Roasters. The company's stated goal is to "provide you with an extraordinary coffee experience that's environmentally sound, socially just, and undeniably delicious."[11] The integration of the company's values with its innovative business model and corporate partnerships has lead to its recognition as one of the leaders in corporate social responsibility. Green Mountain Coffee Roasters does this by setting clear expectations for its suppliers in terms of wages, benefits, labor rights, health, safety, and environmental responsibility. The company has the same high expectations for its manufacturers and corporate partners.

In other cases, market conditions partially support the activities of the social venture. *Market-augmented social enterprises* benefit from the revenue generation of their products and services, but do not attain sufficient revenues to provide competitive returns to investors. Often, altruistic founders and investors are willing to exchange these lower rates of return for the intrinsic satisfaction associated with providing for the public good. In other cases, the social enterprise requires some support from government agencies or charitable contributions. Husk Power Systems is an example of the market-augmented social enterprise. Funded by donations, impact investors, and venture capital, this innovative company specializes in decentralized generation and distribution of electric power through the use of biomass waste, predominantly discarded rice husks. The company uses this agricultural waste to generate electricity in over sixty "mini-power plants" located throughout rural India. As a result, approximately 25,000 households in over 250 villages now have access to electric power. Moreover, each power plant replaces approximately 42,000 liters of kerosene and 18,000 liters of diesel per year, making the company's solution not just better for the people it serves, but also for the overall global population as a result of the positive environmental impact Husk Power creates.[12]

Extra-market social enterprises provide goods and services from which they are unable to generate significant revenues. Extra-market social enterprises exist where market failures are pervasive and not subject to alteration. They typically arise to fill market needs where direct economic incentives fail to support value creation. They often operate as nonprofits and are reliant upon subsidies in the form of donations or government support. While not financially driven by markets, they nonetheless can be viable, financially sustainable ventures and provide for the public good. Among the countless examples of extra-market social enterprises, one that stands out is Trees, Water & People (TWP). TWP has developed a community-based approach to sustainable international development, specializing in reforestation, watershed protection, renewable energy, clean cook stoves, ecosystem restoration, and education programs in Latin America and the United States.[13] TWP engages local citizens to play an active role in the care and management of their natural resources. As a result, the company preserves local ecosystems and creates social and economic well-being in the community.

Market-convergent social enterprises are actively engaged in the process of altering market institutions and incentive systems to enable their social missions. Such entrepreneurs understand market dynamics and transform markets to better serve the public good and attain competitive returns for their owners and investors. As discussed in earlier chapters such social entrepreneurs may be seen as institutional entrepreneurs who eliminate the conditions of market failure through new property rights, political, legal, or contracting structures. They create an environment for profitable business models by operating in a more socially and environmentally sustainable manner.

COMPETING AS A SOCIAL ENTERPRISE

Competing directly with traditional profit-maximizing firms can be a challenge for many social ventures. Commercial enterprises can easily tell if they are meeting consumer needs because there are clear market signals. That is, if consumers like and accept the product or service that a firm is offering, then they exchange money for said product or service. However, it is more difficult for a social venture to tell if it is meeting its goals for two reasons: (1) because of blurry or nonexistent market signals and (2) because part of the value proposition is judged by other stakeholders that may have a different value system.

Regarding market signals, there may not yet exist a system by which the market indicates a willingness to pay for the product or service that is being offered by the social venture. This is especially true when the product or service is traditionally seen as something to which everyone is entitled, is free, or is something that people are not accustomed to paying for.

Moreover, developing metrics for assessing social and environmental value creation is inherently challenging.[14] Even as one is able to measure impact, it remains difficult to express that effect in financial terms: What is the value of reducing pollution in a given watershed, of reducing homelessness in an inner city, or of providing better nutrition for children in poor countries? Traditional markets do not do a good job of signaling an appropriate value.[15] For example, experts are now trying to quantify the value of ecosystem services. However, for most of recent history, people around the world have expected the services that the Earth naturally provides to be free. We now see that as we impact, interrupt, and change global ecosystems, we can no longer take for granted the benefits that nature provides to various enterprises and society in general. However, the market for paying for these ecosystem services remains in an embryonic stage because the global market has not traditionally engaged in this type of exchange, which makes the market signals blurry and sometimes confusing.

Market signals can be mixed not only based on relative newness, but also because in the social sector there may be value judgments associated with the product or service that make implementing on a wide scale challenging. For example, an entity that is created to combat unwanted pregnancy and curb the spread of sexually transmitted diseases by promoting safe sex might be opposed by certain religious organizations and individuals that do not subscribe to the same value system. In such cases, social entrepreneurs need to understand whether they are truly meeting a social need and whether there is enough support for their work to make it a scalable and impactful venture. If the social venture is at odds with the value system of the community it is trying to serve, it may be challenging to make a lasting positive impact.

The entrepreneur must also be keenly aware that the value system of one population may not be shared with another and should be careful to create a social venture that is aligned with stakeholder values. It is also important to recognize that he or she might not have all the answers, and while the entrepreneur's intentions may be pure, there might be unintended consequences of his or her actions in the social sector. This is especially true in developing countries, where the entrepreneur may not be aware of some of the customs, norms, values, and economic systems that influence daily life. Many development projects have failed over the long run because they did not take the long-term viability of the project into consideration.

Imagine a rural African village that does not have running water. Then a social enterprise comes in and offers to drill a well. Running water is provided, and people are happy. It seems like the social need has been addressed, so the well-intentioned well driller moves onto the next village. Some time later, the well pump breaks in the first village and there is no equipment or expertise to fix it, so it sits unused and does not create any value. Unfortunately, we have seen too much aid work done in this fashion. By looking solely at the social need, we may develop the mindset that people and communities are deficient and take on a paternalistic role rather than a partnering role. To avoid the trap of paternalistic development, one can contrast the social need concept by working with assets (human, environmental, economic, etc.) that already exist in the community and giving the stakeholders a say in how the social venture will most positively impact their lives and be sustainable. By understanding what a person, entity, or community has to offer, we have a better chance of partnership and leveraging existing assets to truly meet a social need. This concept is critical for developing innovative ideas for value creation in social entrepreneurship.

CREATING SHARED VALUE IN SOCIAL ENTREPRENUERSHIP

Value creation is an important part of any sustainable venture. Just as commercial enterprises create economic value, the sustainable and social entrepreneur also seeks to create social or environmental value for society. Conceiving a way to measure the value created and to monetize its value is a constant challenge for social and sustainable entrepreneurs and larger companies alike.

The emerging concept of *shared value,* introduced by Harvard Business School professor and management guru Michael Porter, emphasizes how a company's value proposition to the market has begun to include a focus on the connections between societal and economic progress. Shared value can be defined as "policies and operating practices that enhance the competitiveness of a company while simultaneously advancing economic and social conditions in the communities in which it operates."[16] This leading-edge concept helps drive companies like Google, IBM, Intel, Wal-Mart, and other multinational corporations (MNCs) to reposition themselves in the market via a change in their value proposition to include social and environmental value creation rather than merely economic value creation. Firms can create shared value opportunities in three ways: (1) reconceive products and markets, (2) redefinine productivity, and (3) enable local cluster development.[17]

Reconceive Products and Markets

Product development for new and existing markets is a rapidly growing and dynamic field. Designers, marketers, aid agencies, large companies, small enterprises, and entrepreneurs from all realms are constantly looking for new products to better serve consumers' needs. As globalization continues at a breakneck pace, this means that all of the aforementioned entities can literally look worldwide for their consumer base. For many businesses, this means rethinking their products for varied cultures, climates, social structures, distribution channels, and price points.

One multinational corporation (MNC) that rethought its product for a new market is Unilever, a company specializing in nutrition, hygiene, and personal care items. The company wanted to open up a new market by moving into India, but found that most people in the more economically constrained areas could not afford to purchase a full bottle of shampoo. Such a purchase could require all the cash a family had for the week. That is not to say that this market segment cared any less about personal hygiene; the shampoo was simply packaged in too great a volume for it to be a reasonable purchase. Because the common view held that this market was too poor to afford these products, the population was woefully underserved by large and small companies alike. Contrary to the general thinking at the time, the Indian branch of Unilever, Hindustan Lever, saw this underserved market as a major opportunity and created single-serve packages of shampoo and sold them through small village vendors that traditionally supply similar products. By rethinking their product for a previously underserved market, Hindustan Lever was able to significantly expand its reach, delivering value to both the company and the population it serves.[18]

Redefine Productivity

In the same way that rethinking products and markets can have a great impact on a company and a consumer base, redefining productivity can also lead to shared value creation. The shared-value model contends that if a company optimizes profits in the context of creating additional value for society, then the company can increase its profitability. The model of short-term profit maximization for a firm sometimes runs contrary to creating societal benefit because many have looked at doing good for society (e.g., adding environmental controls, hiring underserved populations, or implementing safety procedures) as a constraint or cost to a corporation. A company focused solely on trying to maximize its short-term profitability may view contributing to society only as raising costs and decreasing profits.

Recall the concept of negative externalities, which exist when societal costs are created by a firm that it does not have to bear. Instead society at large absorbs the costs. In order to make a company, or an industry for that matter, more accountable for the costs it imposes on society, governments often regulate or tax activities that cause externalities. Companies often see this type of regulation as an additional cost of doing business and as something that detracts from their profitability. Stuart Hart, a thought leader in social and sustainable enterprise, calls this the "Great Trade-off Illusion": "the belief that firms must sacrifice performance to meet societal obligations."[19] As companies are forced to internalize externalities, it is no wonder that many of them view social and environmental responsibility as an unnecessary cost and discount these issues from their financial strategies. Furthermore, many companies have ceded the problems to governments and nonprofit entities. However, as we learned earlier in the book, with the existence of externalities come opportunities. As corporations find ways to increase productivity and profitability by creating shared value, they will likely be in a better position than those that continue to pit profit against society and the environment.

Enable Local Cluster Development

The third way to create shared value within a community is to foster economic cluster development. Michael Porter defines *clusters* as "geographic concentrations of interconnected companies, specialized suppliers, service providers, and associated institutions in a particular field that are present in a nation or region."[20] Examples of clusters in the United States include Detroit's auto industry and Silicon Valley's high-tech industry. Of course, there are many other examples in a wide variety of geographies and industry sectors. The basic goal of cluster development is to increase productivity for the firms operating within that industry sector through shared access to a talent pool, suppliers, and in-depth industry expertise that is not easily found or replicated in other areas.

By supporting the growth of industry clusters, a community can create economic growth, open new markets, and reduce business costs. This is important for all entrepreneurs, social or otherwise, because, as we know, an entrepreneur must be skilled at amassing and aligning resources to get ventures off the ground and grow them successfully. By knowing what industry clusters and expertise exist in the community, one can find and exploit resources to do more with less, as well as create additional value through positive interactions with other businesses, governments, nonprofits, and individuals. The idea of partnering with other entities for win–win collaborations is powerful in today's economy. If additional value can be created through meaningful business partnerships, then it is a win for all parties involved.

By incorporating at least one of the three approaches to the shared-value concept in business development, a social venture can realize new opportunities to generate increased innovation, stronger company growth, and societal benefits.[21] This is particularly valuable to social entrepreneurs, as their venture structure is defined by their interest in creating social value and finding solutions to some of societies most pressing issues.

BASE OF THE PYRAMID MARKETS FOR SOCIAL ENTREPRENEURS

Interest in the study of social entrepreneurship grows as global communities awaken to the idea that social entrepreneurship is as vital to preserving and enhancing the health of our societies as traditional commercial entrepreneurship is imperative to increasing our economic vitality.[22] Across the globe, many people live on less than $2,000/year, and some on less than that.[23] This massive sector of the economy is called the *base of the pyramid (BOP)*. Taking ideas and strategies from the entrepreneurial private sector and applying them to social challenges at the BOP is one way to make positive change in the world and have a lasting impact on the global community. Indeed, there is a powerful role for social entrepreneurs and larger MNCs to serve the base of the pyramid and make real economic and social change in markets all over the globe.

This is not charity work. Real and viable markets exist even in the poorest of places. However, they may need to be addressed differently. The common misconception is that poor people do not have money to invest in things that add value to their lives. As C. K. Prahalad has explained, "While individual incomes may be low, the aggregate buying power of poor communities is actually quite large."[24] For example, individuals in developing countries are avid consumers of mobile telecommunications, and countries like India, South Africa, and Bolivia have witnessed a telecom boom. In BOP markets, an entrepreneurial approach is necessary to identify opportunities that others do not see. Although it may be necessary to approach these markets in a different way, such an approach can be quite profitable, as it has for some of the world's largest telecommunication providers.

The idea of social entrepreneurship in the BOP is not lost on large MNCs. In fact, many large companies stand to benefit from a social entrepreneurial approach if they can find yet undiscovered ways to create value for customers. BOP population segments are generally not integrated into the global market economy and therefore do not benefit from it. As a result, BOP populations have significant unmet needs and have a dependence on informal (outside of the formal and or legal economy) or subsistence livelihoods.[25]

Of course, there are concerns about entrepreneurial ventures and large companies entering impoverished markets and exploiting the poor. This leads to an debate about how this can be done in the most effective, efficient, and profitable way for social entrepreneurs. For example, is it fair for a microfinance organization to break into a market and provide a loan that has a 20 percent annual interest rate (which is usury by many people's standards), when the customer is used to paying a 50 percent or 100 percent annual rate? If the service adds value to the customer, it can be a win–win. That is not to say that no ethical questions need to be asked, but the fact remains that there is great room for innovation in BOP markets, and social entrepreneurs are leading the way.

Economically depressed nations continue to be overlooked as cradles of innovation, but that is changing as the world flattens and more people have access to better and more reliable information. The for-profit and nonprofit social sectors have vast potential to grow into developing nations and create tremendous value for millions, if not billions, of people. There are many ways to address the global challenges our world is facing, and many types of ventures and business models that can achieve powerful results.

Summary

The concept of social entrepreneurship was borne of the idea that there is a more effective and efficient way of addressing the pressing global challenges of our time. In very broad terms, a social venture may be viewed as an organization that seeks to create social value through innovative products, services, or business models. Social entrepreneurship can be distinguished from other enterprises by the venture's prioritization of social value creation over the generation of personal or organizational financial wealth. While debates remain over the exact definition of social entrepreneurship, many experts agree that social entrepreneurship employs the ideas and tools traditionally used by entrepreneurs in the private sector.

As the earlier examples illustrate, there is opportunity in social entrepreneurship. From small localized nonprofits to revolutionary global corporations, businesses are finding and making opportunities to become more competitive by creating shared value and win–win scenarios from which both businesses and society benefit. The growing excitement in this field is evident in the burgeoning number of community, academic, and professional organizations that are fostering and promoting social entrepreneurship models as a means of creating economic opportunity while addressing the challenges of local and global communities. What's more, some of the largest and wealthiest business people and corporations in the world are adding financial horsepower to this effort. With the infusion of expertise and capital, there is undoubtedly a tremendous amount of opportunity in the field of social entrepreneurship.

Key Learnings

1. *Social entrepreneurship* embraces innovation, revenue-generating business models, and enterprise skills to solve local and global challenges such as poverty, disease, inequity, the lack of education, and environmental degradation.
2. As a concept, social entrepreneurship is distinguished by the entrepreneur's mission to create social value and the prioritization of social value creation over the generation of personal or organizational financial wealth.
3. Social ventures include both for-profit and nonprofit organizations and have been classified into *nonprofit social ventures*, *hybrid nonprofit social ventures*, and for-profit *social business ventures*.
4. Social ventures may also be classified according to the nature of the market conditions, which include *market-driven, market-augmented, extra-market, and market-convergent* enterprises.
5. Social ventures can succeed at creating shared value by reconceiving products and markets, redefining productivity, and enabling local cluster development.
6. Social entrepreneurs often address challenges in base of the pyramid markets, markets in which individuals live on less than $2000 per year.

Endnotes

1. G. J. Dees, 2001, "The Meaning of Social Entrepreneurship," http://www.caseatduke.org/documents/dees_sedef.pdf, p. 2, accessed February 7, 2013.

2. United Nations, 2012 Millenium Goals, http://www.un.org/millenniumgoals/bkgd. shtml, accessed January 20, 2012.

3. Ashoka Innovators for the Public, "Vision and Mission," available online at: https://www.ashoka.org/visionmission, accessed February 7, 2013.

4. Ashoka Innovators for the Public, "Approach," available online at: https://www.ashoka.org/approach, accessed February 7, 2013.

5. Acumen Fund, "About Us," available online at: http://www.acumenfund.org/about-us.html, accessed February 7, 2013.

6. J. Elkington and P. Hartington, *The Power of Unreasonable People* (Boston: Harvard Business Press, 2008).

7. "Habitat for Humanity Fact Sheet," Habitat for Humanity, http://www.habitat.org/how/factsheet.aspx, accessed January 30, 2012.

8. "One for One, Tom's, http://www.toms.com/our-movement/movement-one-for-one, accessed February 7, 2013.

9. K. Westaway, "New Legal Structures for "Social Entrepreneurs," *Wall Street Journal*, December 12, 2011, available online at: http://online.wsj.com/article/SB10001424052970203413304577088604063391944.html, accessed February 7, 2013.

10. The Economist, "B Corps: Firms with Benefits: A New Sort of Caring, Sharing Company Gathers Momentum," Print Edition. January 7, 2012, available online at: http://www.economist.com/node/21542432/print, accessed January 24, 2013.

11. GMCR, "Building a Better World," available online at: http://gmcr.com/brewing-a-better-world.html, accessed February 7, 2013.

12. Husk Power Systems, "Community Impact," available online at: http://www.huskpowersystems.com/innerPage.php?pageT=Community%20Impact&page_id=81, accessed February 7, 2013.

13. Trees, Water & People Home Page, available online at: http://www.treeswaterpeople.org, accessed February 7, 2013.

14. Dees, "The Meaning of "Social Entrepreneurship,"

15. Ibid.

16. M. Porter and M. Kramer, M., "Creating Shared Value," *Harvard Business Review* 89 nos. 1/2 (2011): 62–77.

17. Ibid.

18. C. K. Prahalad, *The Fortune at the Bottom of the Pyramid: Eradicating Poverty Through Profits* (Upper Saddle River, NJ: Wharton School Publishing, 2006).

19. S. Hart, *Capitalism at the Crossroads: Aligning Business, Earth, and Humanity* (Upper Saddle River, NJ: Wharton School Publishing, 2007).

20. M. Porter, "Clusters and the New Economics of Competition," *Harvard Business Review* 76, no. 6 (1998): 77–90.

21. M. Porter and M. Kramer, M., "Creating Shared Value."

22. J. Thompson, "Social Enterprise and Social Entrepreneurship: Where Have We Reached?: A Summary of Issues and Discussion Points," *Social Enterprise Journal* 4 (2008): 149–161.

23. C. K. Prahalad, *The Fortune at the Bottom of the Pyramid: Eradicating Poverty Through Profits* (Upper Saddle River, NJ: Wharton School Publishing, 2006).

24. Ibid.

25. A. Hammon, W. Kramer, R. Katz, J. Tran, and C. Walker, *The Next 4 Billion: Market Size and the Business Strategy at the Base of the Pyramid,* World Resources Institute and International Finance Corporation, 2007, available online at: http://www.wri.org/publication/the-next-4-billion, accessed February 7, 2013.

CHAPTER 5

ENVIRONMENTAL MARKETING AND THE GREEN CUSTOMER

INTRODUCTION

The potential for marketing the environmental attributes of products is substantial. Practiced well, it can lead to competitive advantage for the sustainable entrepreneur and be a central part of a company's brand and value proposition. Practiced poorly, it can lead to disappointing results, or worse, consumer backlash. Think about the myriad companies and products that have "gone green" in recent years in order to provide additional value for the consumer and capture greater market share in their industry.

The good news for the environmental entrepreneur is that the green consumer segment holds strong values and beliefs that drive purchasing behaviors. Many companies have learned how to identify this buyer, communicate environmental benefits, and build successful product lines and businesses that cater to this segment. But the most successful have learned to transcend the niche market for green products by creating products that deliver both environmental and functional value. Others have learned that authenticity in environmental performance and claims is critical to successful environmental marketing because consumers may eventually see through inauthentic messaging, false environmental claims, and "green-washing." Many of these organizations see their environmental activities and attributes as an important part of a broader brand positioning and that soft-selling those attributes is the best way to delicately navigate the oftentimes rough waters of environmental marketing. Other companies find competitive advantage in marketing to industrial or commercial customers who increasingly monitor the environmental performance of their suppliers.

Environmental (or green) marketing is the marketing of goods and services differentiated by attributes that make those goods beneficial or less harmful to the environment. The theory behind environmental marketing is that environmental attributes will allow the business to charge a higher price for the product, or capture greater market share. When the environmental attribute increases costs of production, that cost must be at least outweighed by the price premium it is able to attain in the marketplace. Otherwise, the added costs of production will place the company at a disadvantage relative to other competitors. When the creation of environmental attributes reduces costs of production, the company may incur a double benefit because doing so both reduces costs and increases the attractiveness of products in the marketplace. In any case, the successful green marketer must (1) find or develop a market that is willing to pay for its environmental attributes, (2) establish the authenticity of its claims through credible information, and (3) be able to defend its uniqueness against competitive imitation.[1]

OPPORTUNITIES FOR ENVIRONMENTAL MARKETING

While many see markets for green products and services as a relatively small niche, opportunities for positioning green products actually span a broad range of potential customers. The key to understanding the nature of these opportunities rests in understanding the value created by offering green products to the consumer and embracing them as part of the value proposition of a new venture. We argue that opportunities for environmental positioning and marketing fall into five categories, reflective of the potential customer base and types of value created for those customers.

The first category is the pure-green consumer, who is fundamentally concerned about environmental issues and the effects of their purchases on the natural environment. The second, typically related to the first, is the group of consumers who look to their green purchases to establish status within their communities and society at large. Such consumers are often interested in sending a signal about their values and communicating to others what is important to them. The third category, which likely holds the greatest potential for green products and services, comes from providing functional value that transcends environmental impacts or status considerations. In other words, creating a product or service that outcompetes similar products in the market *and* has superior environmental performance gives the end user more value, and yields greater economic opportunity for the entrepreneur. Fortunately, green products are often associated with a set of functional value drivers that are attractive to a broad range of consumers. Fourth, many companies and organizations have benefited from environmental strategies that target commercial and industrial customers rather than the final consumer or end user. Indeed, the marketing of green products and services to commercial customers provides a superior opportunity for many environmental entrepreneurs. The fifth and final category is the holistic brand approach, in which the environmental attributes of a company and

TABLE 5.1 Five Opportunities for Environmental Marketing			
Opportunity	*Description*	*Value Drivers*	*Examples*
The Pure-Green Play	Market environmental attributes to consumers concerned about their environmental or social impact	Customer values toward the environment or society	Green Power, Fair-Trade Coffee
Green Status	Market status attributes of green products or services. Customers affiliate with brand or product image	Customer affiliation with brand or product attributes and desire to make a personal statement about priorities	Hybrid electric vehicles, residential solar panels
Functional Value Propositions	Market functional value drivers affiliated with green products	Product quality and performance, efficiency and cost savings, health and safety	High-efficiency clothes washers, organic foods, composite decking, green buildings
Commercial or Industrial Markets	Market green attributes to commercial buyers instead of final consumers	Buyers have better understanding of efficiency or performance gains. Allows buyers to affiliate green purchases with corporate brand image or reduce risk of criticism	Organic cotton, green power, high-efficiency computer servers
The Holistic Brand	Companies create holistic brand affiliated with sustainable practices. Often a subtle, understated approach to marketing.	Consumers respond to overall feel of brand or product. Sustainable activities support larger brand image of quality or performance.	Patagonia, New Belgium Brewery

its products are part of a broader brand positioning. Recall General Electric's "ecomagination" campaign. GE was not simply focused on marketing a specific product or service, but was transforming its entire brand to showcase its dedication to innovative technological solutions that provided value to their customers through environmental and product performance.

OPPORTUNITY #1: THE PURE-GREEN PLAY

The opportunity to market the pure-green attributes of a product or service can be substantial in environmental entrepreneurship because some consumers hold values and beliefs that compel them to pay attention to the environmental impacts of the products they purchase. This *pure-green consumer* has a clear preference for products with lower environmental impact and may be willing to pay more for those attributes, even if those attributes provide no additional value for them beyond lower environmental impact. Practically, a pure-green play is typically mixed with other value attributes, such as status or functional value. In other words, most green products provide value beyond their pure environmental considerations. Theoretically, however it is important to distinguish the pure-green play from other types, because the distinction helps to emphasize a specific buyer behavior that may be addressed by the sustainable entrepreneur.

A great example of a pure-green product is the marketing of renewable energy to consumers. Renewable energy is sold to residential customers through specific green-power marketing programs sponsored by utilities or through independent renewable energy credit providers. Buyers of green power are assured that for every unit of electricity provided to their homes a unit of renewable electricity is added to the grid. In other words, consumers do not get the exact electrons produced by renewable energy sources, but electrons from renewable sources are added to the grid in the amount that they purchase. The structure of these markets is complex, but the extent to which consumers purchase green power is an indication how much they value the pure environmental attributes of what they buy, because they pay more for the assurance that renewable power was produced to offset their use. Penetration rates for green power in residential markets vary greatly by geographic region, but average penetration rates for utility-provided renewable energy in U.S. residential markets was in the neighborhood of 2 percent in 2009, accounting for millions of kilowatt hours.[2] In some regions, penetration rates for utility green pricing programs are higher than 5 percent. On average, customers pay about 1.5 cents more per kilowatt-hour in utility green-pricing programs.[3]

The market for green power demonstrates the willingness of some consumers to purchase the pure-green attributes of products and services. While penetration rates of 2 percent are not high in relative terms, 2 percent of a large market like the United States can be the foundation for a substantial environmental business serving the pure-green niche. Surveys of green consumers often suggest that the percentage of consumers willing to pay more for green attributes is substantially larger, but the difference between what consumers say in these surveys and their actual behavior can be considerable.

The reasons why people buy pure environmental attributes are not entirely clear, but they appear to be at least partially linked to a concern for the welfare of others (perhaps altruism) and values of individual responsibility.[4] In economic terms, such behaviors are termed the *private provision of a public good* because private individuals are paying for the benefit of others (or the environment). The extent to which individuals are willing to provide for the public good should not be underestimated because history has shown a significant willingness to do so in multiple contexts. Charitable donations, volunteer work, and recycling are all behaviors that demonstrate a degree of altruism or individual contributions to society at large. So the potential for marketing pure-green attributes to a significant percentage of the market remains. The key to breaking into a larger segment of the market may lie in positioning those attributes in a way that makes it compelling and accessible to a broader customer base. Moreover, it is important for the company or entrepreneur to understand that the extent to which an individual desires to provide for the public good varies substantially across cultural context, levels of income, and time.

With respect to cultural context, it is clear that some cultures place greater value on individual responsibility to contribute to the broader needs of society. Culture may also affect how those responsibilities materialize into actual buying behavior, as what might be considered responsible behavior in one society may be different in another. With respect to income levels, contributions to the public good might be seen as a luxury,[5] in that the desire to contribute to the public environmental good likely increases disproportionally with income level. In other words, the greater a person's income, the greater the likelihood he or she will spend time or money contributing to public environmental quality. Finally, it is important not to underestimate the extent to which values of individual environmental or social responsibility can vary over time. As the dynamics of media attention, environmental challenges, and scientific information unfold, customer behavior and the desire to purchase environmental attributes can vary substantially. Understanding how social norms and environmental concerns evolve in a society over time is critical to understanding the degree to which customers are willing to pay for environmental attributes they deem important.

However, it is perhaps even more important to understand how environmental attributes might relate to individuals' desire for social status and to the purchase of environmentally superior products to meet those status needs.

OPPORTUNITY #2: SELLING GREEN STATUS

An individual's willingness to purchase environmental attributes in products may also be driven by the desire for social status, which has been a useful tool in selling a wide variety of goods or services that increase one's self-image and sense of how others perceive them. Of course, fulfilling an individual desire for an affiliation with environmental attributes can be a powerful marketing strategy. Just as customers are attracted to the affiliations they receive from the purchase of a designer purse, a luxury vehicle, or a large house, some customers want to send a green signal through their purchases. This signal appears related to their desire to send a message about their priorities, but may also serve to show others how thoughtful they are about the state of the world or how savvy they are about cutting-edge technology. The success of the Toyota Prius hybrid electric vehicle is a case in point. Although the vehicle clearly has other advantages, many drivers have embraced the image associated with the vehicle, an image that could speak to concern for both the environment and for dependence on foreign oil.[6] The rising interest in green homes and solar energy panels may also stem from owners taking pride in their sustainable practices.

The irony of using green purchases to demonstrate a personal commitment to the environment is not lost on many observers. Purchasing more products and increasing consumption may not be the most effective approach to environmentalism, but at least it may be argued that, in comparison to other consumptive alternatives, there is lower environmental impact from many green products.

Selling to image-conscious green consumers bears some similarity to selling to those interested in the pure-green attributes of products in that societal values, timing, and positioning matter a great deal. Interest in the Toyota Prius, for example, was generated by a combination of rising gasoline prices, increasing concern for climate change, and energy security issues. In addition, the ability to purchase costly status symbols tends to be correlated with income level. And, of course, positioning a green product properly in the minds of a consumer base is absolutely critical to success. In the end, it may be difficult to distinguish whether buyers act out of altruism or the desire to increase social status, as the two motivations are likely related.

In addition, the environmental entrepreneur reliant on the pure-green and status-conscious green consumer may experience rapid decreases (or increases) in market demand. Indeed, while many entrepreneurs have been pleasantly surprised by the response of these markets, others have experienced disappointments. The pure-green and green-status markets have proven fickle because they are driven by attitudes, incomes, and contextual factors. This is particularly true when the green product has a higher price, lower quality, or does not provide additional customer value.

Green-marketing myopia occurs when businesses focus too much on the pure-green and status-attributes of their products, without considering important value drivers that increase the attractiveness of their offerings.[7] Fortunately, avoiding green-marketing myopia can be achieved by focusing marketing efforts on the numerous value-drivers inherent to many green products.

OPPORTUNITY #3: FUNCTIONAL VALUE PROPOSITIONS

A superior approach to environmental marketing may be to understand, offer, and promote functional value attributes that are associated with a green product. In other words, creating and marketing functional customer benefits that go beyond the pure-green and status attributes of green products is more likely to be effective with a broader audience. This strategy has proven successful, if not transformative, in numerous industries from organic foods to green buildings.

This approach is attractive for three primary reasons. First, it broadens the target market for green products and services beyond the niche of the pure or status-conscious green consumer and expands the potential of a venture significantly, as mainstream consumers become more likely customers. Second, this strategy is more resilient to changes in customer attitudes toward green products because it provides a superior offering without reliance on green claims. Third, customer benefits are often embedded in greener products simply because of the nature of the products themselves. Indeed, many green products are not of inferior quality (a criticism of many of them in the past), but instead offer superior quality and other benefits that enhance their value to customers. Customer benefits may include increased efficiency and cost effectiveness, health and safety, convenience, and better overall quality and performance.[8]

Increased *efficiency and cost effectiveness* are primary drivers of demand for green products. The most prominent efficiency in green products is probably enhanced energy efficiency. Internet service providers (ISPs) have realized the tremendous energy consumption necessary to maintain large banks of computer servers. To make matters worse, the server banks create heat, which increases the need for air conditioning in facilities. Combined, the electricity needed to run and cool the servers is an increasingly important aspect of ISP businesses. Server manufacturers have recognized the problem and begun to design more efficient servers and to promote the energy savings associated with their devices. The market for light bulbs is increasingly driven by the desire for decreased energy usage, and the demand for compact fluorescent and LED lighting is expanding rapidly as a result. The same is true for a host of other products that reduce energy costs, including green buildings, hybrid electric vehicles, and home appliances.

Cost effectiveness in environmental products may span various stages in the life cycle of a product. First, reducing the energy use, materials consumption, or waste generation in the processes of production can reduce the initial cost of the product to the consumer. Second, reducing the costs of distribution and sale can also affect total costs and reduce the price the consumer pays for a green product. Ownership and disposal costs are perhaps not as obvious, but they are also sources of opportunity for marketing green products.

Customers pay *ownership costs* to use the product throughout its life (beyond the price they pay for the product itself). Fuel efficiency in vehicles is becoming an increasing consideration as gasoline prices rise. Composite decking companies, such as Trex and TimberTech, combine recycled plastics with sawdust to produce a decking material that never needs to be painted or stained. Although more expensive than wood, these products can substantially reduce the costs of labor and ownership. Compact fluorescent and LED bulbs also reduce labor costs, as they need to be replaced less often than standard incandescent bulbs. Digital cameras offer substantially lower ownership and environmental costs relative to film cameras, because the film does not require development with hazardous chemicals.

Disposal costs are costs that customers pay to get rid of a product after its useful life. For businesses, products that contain hazardous wastes can have high disposal costs, particularly when they fall under strict regulatory requirements for handling and disposal. Consumers face both the time involved in disposal and increasing use of quantity based charges for trash disposal in many communities. Disposing of hazardous wastes such as electronics, household chemicals, and paints can require an extra trip to a dedicated disposal facility, as well as charges for disposal of those products.

In purchasing decisions, consumers often overlook ownership and disposal costs. But companies increasingly succeed at marketing lower ownership costs for items like light bulbs that have to be replaced less often. In addition, the amount of attention paid to such costs is greater the more significant the cost is to the buyer. Customers who buy in volume, or for whom the product represents a significant portion of their total costs, are likely to put more effort into estimating the costs of ownership and disposal.

Health and safety attributes have also been one of the primary drivers of the demand for green products. Organic foods are probably the clearest example. As consumers have become increasingly concerned with the use of chemicals in agricultural production, organic foods have provided an alternative that precludes the use of chemical pesticides, fertilizers, and growth hormones. The sales or organic milk companies like Horizon Organic have benefited substantially by positioning their product as a healthier alternative. While a "good for the planet image" is also affiliated with the brand, mothers are mostly concerned with the health of their children and have helped make Horizon become the leading brand of organic milk in the United States. As concern for indoor air pollution has also increased, marketers of green buildings and green building products have also benefited. From carpets to paints to furniture, manufactures are increasingly offering products that reduce chemicals in the home. As consumers examine such products, lower toxicity is often higher on their priority list than environmental concerns.

Finally, it has become increasing obvious that some green products just *perform better* than their alternatives. First and foremost, customers want products that work and fulfill their needs. Green buildings are some of the highest-performing buildings, not just because they reduce costs of ownership, but also because they provide comfort, superior air quality, natural lighting, and an environment in which people are productive. Newer, front-loading clothes dryers, while being both energy and water efficient, tend to get clothes cleaner and dryer than do the top-loading styles that were standard in the United States for decades. Local and organic foods are often reported as fresher and better tasting than nonlocal and traditionally grown alternatives.

Combined, these functional value propositions for a wide variety of green products have increased the opportunities available to the environmental entrepreneur. Marketing green products has evolved from a narrow pursuit, focused on convincing a niche market to buy green for the sake of green, into a complex yet vibrant activity in which the functional benefits of green products are recognized and promoted to a broad audience. Whether selling pure green, green status, functional benefits, or an innovative combination of all these, the opportunities available for marketing green products are increasingly attractive.

OPPORTUNITY #4: TARGETING COMMERCIAL AND INDUSTRIAL MARKETS

While most of the attention in environmental marketing focuses on selling to consumers, opportunities exist for promoting green products to commercial and industrial buyers. Indeed many environmental entrepreneurs have benefited much more from commercial markets than from consumer markets. For example, Aurora Organic Dairy manufactures private label milk that is sold under the brands of national grocery stores and other retailers. Renewable Choice Energy started by marketing renewable-energy credits to homeowners, but soon found that large customers like Vail Resorts, Whole Foods, and various green builders accounted for an increasing percentage of their sales. Solar power installers like Powerlight (now owned by SunPower) have focused on large commercial installations instead of residential customers, as such customers can deal much more effectively with the complexities of installations and the transaction costs of each installation are likely much lower.

Marketing green products to commercial customers has a number of advantages. First, for commercial and industrial customers, cost is critical. To the extent that green products increase energy efficiency or otherwise lower costs, they can be very attractive. VanDyne SuperTurbo, an engine-efficiency venture, plans to sell its products and technology to manufacturers of on-highway truck engines. In these markets, vehicle fuel-efficiency is crucial and even small gains in efficiency are highly valued. In addition, because purchases are completed in larger quantities, commercial customers may put more effort into learning about the attributes of various products. When selling a product with unique and new attributes, the entrepreneur may be best served by targeting customers who understand the product or are willing to put the time in to learn about its advantages. Hazardous waste rules in commercial enterprises may also be much stricter and therefore more costly. Products that provide alternatives to the use of hazardous substances can reduce these costs and be attractive to such customers.

But perhaps most importantly, commercial and industrial customers increasingly view their supply chain as an opportunity either to enhance their green image or to reduce their risk of criticism for purchasing from environmentally or socially deficient suppliers. One of Patagonia's most important environmental initiatives was to adopt the use of organic cotton in all its products. Since the organic cotton industry was pretty much nonexistent at the time, this created substantial opportunities for those interested in creating the additional supply. Commercial buyers of wind power increased rapidly after a few high-profile companies committed to be 100 percent wind powered. Often, such actions are part of a larger corporate strategy to enhance sustainability and develop an environmental image. But perhaps most importantly, large retailers like Wal-Mart have made substantial commitments to examine the sustainability of their suppliers and increasingly demand environmental metrics and performance from the companies that sell to them. While many companies may view this as a threat, an entrepreneurial firm may see an opportunity to differentiate its products to the world's largest retailers.

OPPORTUNITY # 5 – THE HOLISTIC BRAND

Many environmental entrepreneurs have chosen a completely different path to the idea of environmental marketing. Rather than promoting their environmental attributes directly, they are much more subtle. While they are happy for the occasional press release, they choose to not aggressively promote their activities or the environmental attributes of their products. Interestingly, these companies have some of the most authentic values-driven businesses, active environmental programs, and impressive environmental performance in their industries. They may achieve a sense of doing the right thing and behaving in accordance with their values, but it is also often the case that they are building a brand image to which environmental considerations are central. Thus, they prioritize the quality of their product in their promotional efforts, and soft-sell their environmental action and performance. And, most important, their environmental performance and activities help create and support a holistic brand image that is consistent with their product and business strategy.

One such company is New Belgium Brewing, located in Fort Collins, Colorado. Known for their high-quality, Belgian-style beers with a fun and festive air, New Belgium has been an industry leader in wind-power adoption, water and energy efficiency, and waste disposal. Although not aggressively promoted, their environmental efforts are widely known to their loyal customer base and an inherent part of their brand image. Another company that fits this model is Patagonia. Although their activities are about as authentic as it gets, their promotional efforts often focus more on the quality of their product than on their environmental performance. Nevertheless. the brand stands by their environmental values and actions, and customers are often loyal to them for that reason.

This approach is both subtler and more holistic than other approaches to environmental marketing. The key seems to lie in understanding the complex relationships between environmental attributes of a product, a company, and brand image. By combining high-quality products with authentic environmental and social behaviors, these companies appear to be able to build trust and customer loyalty. They also often serve markets that value environmental performance, such as the market for outdoor recreational apparel.

ESTABLISHING CREDIBLE INFORMATION

Like it or not, one of the realities of green marketing is that consumers tend to distrust green claims. This distrust likely emerges from a general tendency of consumers to question corporate promotion, but it also results from plenty of green-marketing attempts that have been criticized or shown to be false. *Greenwashing* is a popular term that refers to attempts to market a company or its products as environmental when they are not, or at least not perceived to be so. Potential criticism for green claims is a reason to be careful with product and corporate claims and why many companies are hesitant to promote their environmental activities. Environmental entrepreneurs also need to exercise care in their environmental marketing activities.

For their part, green consumers want credible and readily available information on green products and companies in order to make decisions about them. And environmental entrepreneurs wishing to address green markets usually want customers to have credible information about their products and processes.

One way of communicating environmental attributes is through *certification and labeling* programs, which we introduced in Chapter 3. Certification and labeling programs for environmental attributes are widespread, although not as popular as some would prefer. Certification programs for social criteria are also popular, the best known of which is probably fair trade. Certification and labeling programs are typically voluntary, meaning that companies may choose whether or not to participate. *Certification* refers to a process put in place to verify that a product or company meets certain requirements. Industry groups or partnerships between industry, nonprofit organizations, and governments develop the requirements (standards) for certification. *Third-party auditors*, who are independent from the company being certified, typically perform certification. Self-certification may also be allowed, but it typically implies less credibility than systems that require a third party to perform the audits.

Companies typically pursue certification in order to help sell a product, and most certification systems allow and encourage certified companies to promote their certification through labeling. *Eco-labels* are placed on a product to promote its environmental attributes and are often associated with a certification scheme. Eco-labels may be of three general types. *Single-attribute* labels promote a specific environmental feature of a product. One popular type of single attribute label is the percent of recycled content in a product. Single attribute claims are often, but not always, made without third-party certification.

The second type of label is a *seal of approval,* a logo that can be placed on a product or its packaging upon approval by the certifying organization. Seals of approval generally incorporate a number of environmental attributes and are meant to imply that a given product is environmentally superior to others in a particular category. Germany's Blue Angel eco-label is one such seal of approval, as is the U.S. Energy Star label for appliances. The European Union also sponsors an eco-labeling program called the EU Ecolabel. Seals of approval may be *generic* and cross multiple products, or be *specific* to a particular industry or sector. Germany's Blue Angel and the EU Ecolabel are examples of generic labels because they are applicable across a broad set of products and industries, ranging from tissue paper to detergents to electronics. For each product category, the schemes develop criteria by which they evaluate and approve specific products. Green-e, developed and managed by the nonprofit Center for Resource Solutions, is a good example of an industry-specific seal of approval. Green-e evaluates and approves renewable energy credits for sale to those interested in purchasing renewable electricity. The Green-e logo communicates to buyers that the renewable energy credit they are purchasing meets their standards.

The third type of label is an *eco-profile,* which is in a report card format similar to nutritional labels on food. Rather than a single seal or logo, the eco-profile lists various environmental attributes and the relevant measures of how the product scores on those attributes. The shoe company Timberland has been labeling some of its products with its Green Index profile label and is promoting the adoption of a similar label (the Eco-Index) by the outdoor products industry. The Green Index rates the company's products on climate impact, chemicals used, and resource consumption. Eco-profile labels offer the benefit of specific measurements on a product's impact and allow the consumer to decide which attributes are most important to them. But such labels can also be more difficult to interpret because there is more data than on a single seal of approval, and because the trade-offs between various attributes can be unclear to consumers.

For any certification and labeling program, there are often challenges and trade-offs in determining how to rate products within each category. One of the primary challenges rests in establishing the criteria by which certification and approval is determined. This process can be complex and involve multiple constituencies. It can also be expensive. Furthermore, substantial trade-offs can exist in determining the criteria. Broadly speaking, the systems need to determine relative trade-offs between such measures as the chemical constituents, climate impacts, pollutant emissions, energy efficiency, and material consumption. Arriving at a single number on environmental impact is also nearly impossible because of these trade-offs. Determining what is important is often a matter of priorities.

In addition, different stakeholders in the development of the criteria may not share the same priorities, particularly when one group or company stands to gain competitive edge based on the standards. Competitive battles about criteria may emerge, with some participants hoping to promote their particular strengths through the process.

While some may not view a particular product category to be at all environmental (i.e., a two-stroke engine leafblower), certifying programs are nonetheless interested in determining which products within that category are environmentally superior to others. So comparisons within a particular product category are often important and the only way forward in some categories. Thus, certification may not imply that the particular category is superior, but rather that among the products within that category, certain products are merely preferable.

Furthermore, environmental impact occurs across the entire life cycle of the products' use, from raw material extraction to customer use to final disposal. Calculating impacts across the entire life cycle is difficult. *Life cycle analysis (LCA)* is a procedure that attempts to inventory all of the impacts across the life of a product in order to determine its total environmental impact. It is an expensive methodology. Even if completed, decisions have to be made on the boundary conditions for the inventory and relative priorities of various impacts. LCA is nonetheless being used increasingly to measure, understand, and improve the environmental impacts of products. However, most certification systems and companies do not have the financial resources to pursue complete life cycle analyses for products.

Governments can, and often do, aid in the development of certification and labeling programs. Governments can help establish processes and standards for certification, add legitimacy to programs, and help resolve some of the political issues involved in setting priorities for certification. Germany's Blue Angel, the European Union's Ecolabel, and the United States' Energy Star and organic foods standards are all sponsored and managed by government agencies.

TIPS FOR ENVIRONMENTAL MARKETING

1. *Be Specific.* Broad claims of environmental superiority can be risky. Almost all environmental attributes involve trade-offs, and broad claims of green fail to recognize this fact. As such, general claims may make the company vulnerable to criticism for green-washing, either because the company fails to undertake certain actions or because of the other environmental impacts it creates. The U.S Federal Trade Commission's Guidelines for the Use of Environmental Marketing Claims also emphasizes the need to make specific rather than general claims. These guidelines note that claims overstating environmental benefits may be considered misleading or deceptive. They also suggest that specific information be provided on any qualifications of claims, the basis for comparisons, and whether the claim applies to the product, packaging, or use of the product.[9]

2. *Be Sincere.* In our world of increasing transparency, claims that are not based on authentic action and performance are likely to be the subject of criticism, or even lawsuit. In addition, authenticity in corporate environmental performance is critical to building a brand for an environmental entrepreneur. The lack of sincerity in claims can quickly destroy efforts to build trust with a consumer base. On the other hand, authenticity in green products and corporate action can be critical aspect of branding and building a loyal and energized customer base.

3. *Be Subtle.* As discussed earlier, aggressive marketing campaigns based on green attributes can fail. While you don't want to undersell you environmental benefits, aggressive claims can also result in consumer backlash and can even alienate portions of your customer base that do not hold similar values or have the same priorities. Many companies have been quietly, but authentically, improving their environmental performance. If information is made available, those customers with an interest or passion for these issues can find it. This approach may also include allowing others to speak for you through various environmental awards programs and public relations efforts.

4. *Be Smart.* Avoid green-marketing myopia. Understand that the niche for pure-green and status green products may be an attractive market, but also that it could be limiting. If you can offer functional value, it is better to position your product for its lower costs, increased efficiency, lower toxicity, or superior performance.

Summary

In this chapter we have learned that there are many ways for an entrepreneur or company to capture market share or increase profits through environmental marketing and targeting green customers. Of course, not all customers are driven by environmental factors in their purchasing decisions. However, the market for environmentally friendly goods and services continues to grow and the opportunity in this space is substantial.

There are five categories of opportunities for capitalizing on environmental marketing. The first is selling to the pure-green consumer, who makes purchase decisions based on the environmental impact of products or services. The second is marketing the status that one achieves through the purchase of environmentally responsible products, even if the price is higher than its nongreen counterpart. Some consumers are driven to make decisions based on how they want others to perceive them. The third, and potentially most effective, is the marketing of superior functional value associated with green products—that is, the product or service is better than the competition and delivers superior environmental performance. The fourth category is in the commercial or industrial space—that is, not selling directly to the end user or final consumer, but rather to an entity further upstream in the value chain. Working in commercial markets can represent a substantive opportunity for the sustainable entrepreneur. The fifth category is the holistic approach. Like New Belgium Brewing, some companies live out their environmental ideals in what they do. With the holistic approach, the venture has its environmental ethos engrained in every decision it makes. If executed authentically and well, this approach could drive sales and interest in the company.

No matter the approach taken to promote the environmental attributes of a given product or service, the information that the company puts into public view must be credible and honest. An inauthentic attempt to capture the green market may have severe negative effects and could cause backlash against the company. There are many organizations that certify the environmental claims that a company makes. These certifications can be powerful tools in a consumer's decision-making process, and seeking them out can be rewarding for an entrepreneur.

Key Learnings

1. Environmental (or green) marketing is the marketing of goods and services differentiated by attributes that make those goods beneficial or less harmful to the environment.
2. The theory behind environmental marketing is that environmental attributes will allow the business to charge a higher price for the product, or capture greater market share.
3. The five opportunities for environmental marketing include *The Pure-Green Play, Selling Green Status, Functional Value Propositions, Targeting Commercial or Industrial Markets, and The Holistic Brand.*
4. The pure green play involves marketing to green customers who have a preference for products with lower environmental impact.
5. Selling green status involves marketing to customers who are conscious of their green image and want to make a statement through the products they purchase.
6. Functional value propositions involve offering and promoting superior functional value (utility) to customers. Functional utility is often associated with green products and can include increased efficiency and cost

effectiveness, superior health and safety, or better product quality or performance.

7. Targeting commercial or industrial markets with green products can be highly effective in some sectors, and can have a number of advantages for the sustainable entrepreneur.

8. Some entrepreneurs use environmental attributes of their products and/ or processes to help them create a holistic brand in which those attributes contribute to the company's overall reputation

9. Companies following green or social marketing strategies need to communicate credible information regarding the environmental or social attributes of their products or services. This may be achieved through a myriad of certification and labeling programs.

10. Effective environmental marketing approaches should typically be *specific* (avoid broad claims of green*)*, *sincere* (authentic), *subtle* (not oversold) and *smart* (focus on functional value propositions).

Endnotes

1. F. L. Reinhardt, "Environmental Product Differentiation: Implications for Corporate Strategy," *California Management Review* 40, no. 4 (Summer 1998).
2. L. Bird and J. Sumner, *Green Power Marketing in the United States: A Status Report (2009 Data)*, NREL Technical Report (2010) NREL/TP-6A20-49403.
3. Bird and Sumner, *Green Power Marketing in the United States*.
4. Reinhardt, "Environmental Product Differentiation: Implications for Corporate Strategy."
5. Ibid.
6. J. A. Ottman, E. R. Stafford, and C. L. Hartman, "Avoiding Green Marketing Myopia: Ways to Improve Appeal for Environmentally Preferable Products," *Environment* 48 no. 5 (2006): 296–314.
7. Ibid.
8. Ibid.
9. "Part 260 -- Guidelines for the Use of Environmental Marketing Claims," Federal Trade Commission, http://www.ftc.gov/bcp/grnrule/guides980427.htm, accessed January 13, 2012.

CHAPTER

LAUNCHING THE SUSTAINABLE VENTURE*

INTRODUCTION

Throughout this book we have explored several iconoclastic entrepreneurs whose sustainable ventures have employed traditional and not so traditional business strategies as a vehicle for making positive social and environmental impact. Although no one precise formula can be followed to ensure the success of a sustainable venture, there are indeed recurring elements and activities that are important. In this chapter, we look at six elements essential to launching a sustainable venture. These elements are shown in Figure 6.1 and include *mission, values, plan, legal form, team,* and *metrics.* When implementing a new venture, the entrepreneur should consider each of these elements as they can have lasting effects on the company.

A good place to start is by developing an organization's *mission* and *values*. Mission and values are particularly important in the sustainable venture because social and environmental impacts are often important goals. In addition, an organization's values serve as the foundation for decision-making and the development of business practices. In a well-functioning organization, mission and values are much more than statements—they are an inherent part of the organizational culture, and they drive the company's strategy, tactics, and actions. Moreover, mission and values influence business *planning* and the planning for the specific social and environmental practices that help implement the company's mission. Indeed, what often sets the sustainable venture apart is both

*Jacob T. Castillo was the lead author for this chapter.

FIGURE 6.1 Elements of a Successful Sustainable Venture

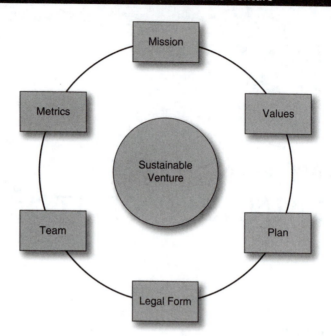

what the company does and the way it does it. A number of unique and emerging *legal forms* of organization are available to the sustainable company. As in most ventures, the members of the *team* are also critical. But in the sustainable venture, the nature of the team is of upmost importance because a values-driven organization will want to attract employees who share some overarching values and goals. Finally, the *metrics* by which an organization evaluates itself need to be considered, particularly when measures of success transcend financial outcomes. In the subsequent sections, we address each of these critical elements to help the sustainable entrepreneur understand the available approaches and activities necessary for success.

MISSION: DEFINE WHY YOU EXIST

In broad terms, a company's mission defines why it exists and encapsulates the unique business in which it operates. Clearly defining your mission will aid in constructing your value proposition and will ultimately drive much of the activity in which the company is involved. By formulating your mission, you define what separates your company from other businesses, particularly if your business has a major social or environmental component. Thus, one should not take the mission development process lightly, as it will help establish the company's identity and focus.

The following are questions you may want to ask yourself and your team as you develop a *mission statement:*

What business am I in?

Why am I in business?

Who are my customers?

What is the image of the company I want to portray?

What is the nature of my product or service?

What sets my company apart from competitors?

What drives my passion for this business?[1]

By the time you are ready to launch the venture, chances are you have already addressed many of these questions. Putting them on paper into a coherent, concise, and effective statement is the next step. The process of crafting the written mission statement will help to solidify the reason for launching a sustainable venture and serve as a powerful tool for showing customers, employees, community, investors, and other businesses what your venture is all about. In a handful of sentences, your mission statement should define the essence of your venture and lay the foundation for further expansion of your value proposition.

The mission statement for a sustainable venture tends to incorporate the fundamental purpose of the venture and has two aspects. The first is the relative prioritization of economic, business, social, and environmental goals. As we have seen, the priorities of sustainable enterprises vary substantially. Some have clear positive effects but are nonetheless primarily driven by financial goals. Others prioritize social or environmental aspects over financial goals. Indeed, a sustainable venture often sets itself apart from traditional companies through an explicit mission to yield positive social and/or environmental impact in the world. Whatever an entrepreneur's particular emphasis, it pays to understand one's goals and priorities and to define why the company exists. This prioritization also helps to calibrate the ethical compass that guides the business through the strategic decisions it faces throughout its lifetime.

With that in mind, the second aspect of the mission that the entrepreneur should consider is the specific social or environmental problem(s) the venture is attempting to address. Social and environmental goals may span a range of issues, from providing low-cost lighting solutions in developing countries that lack power, to providing better educational opportunities in impoverished communities in developed countries, to making nutritious food available in underserved markets in the United States. Indeed, the social and environmental goals of entrepreneurs are diverse in terms of scope, scale, and geography.

As an entrepreneur you might also want to consider whether this mission is achieved primarily through the nature of your product or service and the value it delivers, or through the way you create that service. Greyston Bakery in New York is an interesting example of how social mission is achieved through business practices. Greyston is well known for its brownie products and as the brownie supplier to another sustainably oriented enterprise, Ben & Jerry's Ice Cream. The bakery's mission statement reads: "Greyston Bakery is a force for personal transformation and community economic renewal. We operate a profitable business, baking high quality gourmet products with a commitment to customer satisfaction."[2] In other words, Greyston prioritizes social impact relative to financial goals. Indeed, it focuses on having positive social impact through a profit-driven bakery. In addition, it is not the product itself that creates the positive impact, but, rather, the way that Greyston produces that product; the making of high-quality baked goods is the means to that end.

What sets Greyston apart, aside from its top-quality brownies, is the company's hiring philosophy. Greyston Bakery employs men and women with little to no work experience and has a history of hiring individuals who have been homeless, incarcerated, substance abusers, victims of domestic violence, or illiterate. The profits from the bakery are funneled to the Greyston Foundation, an organization that runs self-sufficiency programs around New York. In addition to Greyston Bakery's formal mission statement, its slogan encapsulates the company's business practices: "We don't hire people to bake brownies. We bake brownies to hire people."[3] Such statements help clarify the scope of the venture, its goals, and objectives. This example also shows that a sustainable venture driven by its mission can have a very compelling and inspiring story. Entrepreneurs can use the development of the mission to help tell their story, share their vision, and gain credibility with stakeholders.

In the end, an organization's mission is its foundation. Taking the time to understand fundamental priorities, market directions, and company orientations is essential to developing a mission. A venture that understands, defines, and communicates its mission builds the foundation for its success, as such efforts help the organization, employees, and external stakeholders act on its priorities and strategic focus.

VALUES: CREATE A CULTURE BASED ON BELIEFS AND PRINCIPLES

As one launches a sustainable venture, it is important to outline the values that will guide the company. *Values* are the principles and philosophies that drive a company's conduct, decision-making, and relationships with external stakeholders.[4] The core values of the sustainable venture affect various facets of the company, from what the company does to its business practices to who it hires. Values statements can deal with human resource issues like diversity or work/life balance or operational concepts such as waste management and environmental stewardship. Understanding its own values helps a company to make strategic decisions as it grows. Commitment to a set of core values helps a company stay true to its mission and identity as it fights its way through the competitive landscape of business in the modern world. As the company matures, these values may be so engrained that they endure, even after an acquisition, buyout, or initial public offering (IPO). Values are particularly important in sustainable ventures, as many sustainable companies are motivated by their values and beliefs rather than by the pursuit of increasing shareholder value. In other cases, a company's values give them an advantage in the marketplace, leading to greater financial success.

New Belgium Brewing is one example of a company strongly committed to its values. When the company was just a concept in the early 1990s, the founders developed a list of values by which they would operate their business. These values are reflected in their current vision, which reads, "To operate a profitable company which makes our love and talent manifest." This vision is accompanied by a ten-item bullet list of the "core values and beliefs" of the company, which all of the employees agree to when they join the company (see Box 6.1). These values continue to serve New Belgium Brewing well today; the company's values are a strong part of its brand image and a point of differentiation in the rapidly expanding craft beer marketplace. It is interesting to note that although New Belgium Brewing has a very real social and environmental component of their operation, they do not lose sight of the economic bottom line in their core values, as stated at the beginning of their vision: "to operate a profitable company. ..."[5]

BOX 6.1 COMPANY VALUES BREWED INTO EVERY BOTTLE . . .

New Belgium Brewing's Core Values and Beliefs

1. Remembering that we are incredibly lucky to create something fine that enhances people's lives while surpassing our consumers' expectations.
2. Producing world-class beers.
3. Promoting beer culture and the responsible enjoyment of beer.
4. Kindling social, environmental and cultural change as a business role model.
5. Environmental stewardship: Honoring nature at every turn of the business.
6. Cultivating potential through learning, high involvement culture, and the pursuit of opportunities.
7. Balancing the myriad needs of the company, our coworkers and their families.
8. Trusting each other and committing to authentic relationships and communications.
9. Continuous, innovative quality and efficiency improvements.
10. Having Fun.

Source: "Our Story," New Belgium Brewing Company, http://www.NewbelgiumBrewing.com/culture/our-story.aspx, accessed January 24, 2013. Used by permission.

Another company that has been successful in incorporating its values into a profitable business model is American Apparel, which began as a designer and manufacturer of soft goods, specializing in T-shirts and similar products. When American Apparel launched, textile and garment production had almost entirely left the United States, and there were growing concerns about sweatshop conditions throughout the garment industry. Stories of dangerous working conditions, extremely long hours, child labor, and sub-subsistence wages began to catch people's attention. At a time when many thought a U.S.-based firm could not compete with the low wages of other countries, American Apparel started a manufacturing operation committed to environmental and employee standards. Its values clearly stated that its garments would be U.S.-made and sweatshop-free.

American Apparel's strategy has paid off. Not only has its message been on point and on trend with a growing demand for U.S.-made products, but its decision to be U.S.-made and sweatshop-free has had material impacts on the company's economic bottom line. Its vertical integration model allows American Apparel to concentrate its entire production into several facilities within only a few square miles of each other in Los Angeles, California. By doing so, the company saves time, money, and fuel costs. The fashion industry moves at a breakneck pace, with new styles coming out every season. American Apparel can be nimble in its production of trendy new styles because its entire design, manufacturing, and distribution team is co-located in the same community.

American Apparel's values drove the company to take big risks in a highly competitive industry. But not all sustainable ventures' values need to mandate risky strategic moves; rather they need to define where the company stands and what the company believes in.

PLAN: IDENTIFY THE ACTIONS TO REACH SUCCESS

President Dwight D. Eisenhower once said, "Plans are worthless, but planning is everything."[6] What he likely meant by this statement is that you can be fairly certain that your plan will not unfold in the way you imagine it. However, the act of planning will give you an advantage in making proper corrections as assumptions or conditions change. A young sustainable venture should recognize that flexibility and adaptability to ever-changing market conditions are necessary in the entrepreneurial journey. Of course, that does not mean you should not plan—quite the contrary—as planning helps the venture team understand market conditions and the actions necessary to achieve organizational goals. In this section we will look at the planning process for implementing a sustainable venture and highlight the primary components of a business plan.

The *What* and the *How*
Good intentions do not always translate into good actions, and it is important that social and environmental entrepreneurs remain focused on their core

mission as they develop their venture plan. This may involve examining both *what* the organization does and *how* it does it. The *what* refers to the type of product or service provided, and sustainable entrepreneurs may ask whether the good or service they provide helps to solve the problems they have committed to solve. The how refers to the manner in which that product or service is created and/or delivered. In other words, the *how* refers to the practices used to create the product or service and whether they achieve certain standards of behavior that might be expected by the organization. Central questions arise about the practices used within the organizational boundaries, such as whether employees are treated fairly and equitably and the methods used in production. Others revolve around where the company sources raw materials, as some companies even extend their values throughout their value chain, encouraging suppliers and customers to meet higher standards.

Thinking back to New Belgium Brewing: their goal, their *what*, so to speak, is making world-class beer. Their *how* is achieved by incorporating environmental sustainability and socially just initiatives throughout their organization and along their value chain. In this example, New Belgium Brewing's means of production and operation makes them a more sustainable venture. There are other examples of entities that could be defined as sustainable ventures based on their core product or service—using the nomenclature from above, their *what*. For example, Envirofit International has a goal of reducing indoor air pollution, and they achieve this is by distributing efficient stoves to underserved markets. Thus, while some organizations may be good at providing a product or service with high social or environmental contribution, others deliver their products and services with processes and operations that exceed the norms for their industries. Hopefully, as organizations continue to learn and allocate scarce resources, they move to solving both the *what* and *how* of their enterprise and to aligning all of their actions and outputs with their social or environmental mission.

Answer the Growth Question

The entrepreneur should also ask himself or herself *if* the company needs to grow, and if so, *why* and by how much. Will growth yield economies of scale in the operation, will it allow the company to have greater social impact, or will it generate more profits? Addressing the growth question up front will help the entrepreneur to focus on the desired scale of the enterprise from the beginning. As we look at some of today's most challenging social and environmental challenges, we see that large scale may be necessary to make positive change. As such, the mission of the sustainable venture will have significant influence over the appropriate size of the company. Regardless, the growth strategy for reaching the desired size of the sustainable venture should be explicit in the business plan.

This is an important factor for the sustainable venture, because bigger does not necessarily mean better. Better means better. And if better means staying small, localized, and ultra-focused, then so be it. But for many sustainable ventures, better also means getting bigger, and the choice for entrepreneurs to grow the company is related to their desire to do more good in the world, just as conventional entrepreneurs may want to grow their business to make more money.[7] Even today, the notion of business growth is sometimes associated with greed, ego, and excessive monetary reward.[8] Although that idea may have some validity, in many cases the need to grow is based on economies of scale within the industry and business sector.[9] Each sustainable venture will be different, so there is no hard-and-fast rule about what the appropriate size is for any given venture.

For example, a sustainable venture committed to bringing local organic food to inner-city Detroit will look different than a company designed to supply affordable eyeglasses to children in impoverished nations, and each of those ventures will have a different scale than a clean-energy company that supplies distributed electrical power to rural communities. Thinking through the appropriate scale of the venture will help in the planning process, especially when looking at the resources needed to accomplish the goals of the venture.

Define Your Value Proposition

With the *what* and the *how* in mind, one of the first steps an entrepreneur should take in the planning of a new venture is to clearly define the *customer value proposition*—that is, how the company's product or service is going to help its customers increase their utility and enhance their life in one way or another. The most successful value propositions come from companies that have identified ways—either through a product or service—to satisfy real customer needs.[10]

Once a company understands its value proposition to the customer and stakeholders, it must formulate a business model that allows the sustainable venture to perpetuate its business and generate value for itself. After all, a sustainable venture that seeks to make the world a better place can only do so if it is financially sustainable. Making sure the business model coincides with the overall value proposition and the business's financial needs is critical. This planning process is the embryonic stage of creating a full-blown business plan, including a financial plan.

Understand Key Resource Needs

In that vein, the next step is to ask what key resources the company will need to fulfill the value proposition? This will help structure resource acquisition strategy and will influence the company's timeline for executing its plan. After all, if the entire venture relies on one crucial item, making sure that one item is in place will determine the viability of the venture. Following are some examples of key resources the entrepreneur may need to launch his or her company:

- Human resources
- Technological resources
- Production or service delivery equipment
- Raw materials
- Facilities
- Distribution channels
- Branding and marketing
- Capital

- Industry networks
- Knowledge and expertise

Once a company has its idea formulated, the value proposition defined, and the resources identified, it is well on its way to starting a business plan.

Develop a Business Plan

The written business plan serves as a guiding roadmap for the implementation and management of the company. Of course, this plan cannot serve as a crystal ball, but it will at least provide an idea of the activities needed for the venture and how they should be used to achieve the company's goals. The reasons for composing a business plan are no different for the sustainable entrepreneur than they are for the traditional entrepreneur, although there are some differences in the content. Sustainable entrepreneurs may want to expound upon their social and environmental mission, practices, and metrics used to evaluate their impact.

There are numerous reasons why an entrepreneur should go through the planning process and write a formal business plan. Perhaps most important, the planning process gives the entrepreneur and the team the chance to think about and address critical strategic questions that the venture will face during the course of operations. Business planning gives entrepreneurs the opportunity to tell their story in a cohesive and meaningful way, weaving together the *what, how, when,* and *how much* of their idea. The planning process also helps define how the company creates value and illustrates how the venture will be a viable enterprise.

The written business plan is also important because it can serve as an introduction to potential investors, funders, business partners, and employees. A strong business plan shows people that you have thought through the many business issues and that a plan exists to make the venture a successful endeavor.[11] A thoughtful and carefully written plan should also show leadership and demonstrate to the employees that the business is sound, has a bright future, and will accomplish its goals if certain milestones are reached.[12] In addition, the business plan can serve as a strategic operating manual for the company and should explicitly outline the actions necessary for the success of the company. Indeed, the plan can serve as a playbook for the operations of the venture as it grows. As part of this, the business plan can identify the key processes that the company can repeat and scale.[13] This could include production, distribution methods, marketing and outreach, employee training, and sales processes. It is important to note that the resources and processes needed to execute the plan are a function of the value proposition and are inextricably linked to the business model. The proper management of resources and processes is the fun and challenging part of launching a sustainable business that creates value to customers, the company, and other stakeholders.[14]

Structure of the Written Business Plan

Now that we understand the reasons for preparing a business plan, let's look at how a business plan is structured and what components need to be included in the plan itself (see Box 6.2).

A business plan typically starts with a *title page* and *table of contents* to show readers what they will find inside. This is usually followed by a two-page *executive summary* of the plan highlighting its salient points and providing a quick synopsis of the business and its potential. Some entrepreneurs find it easier to write the executive summary after the plan is complete since it is a summary of the document. The executive summary should also be crafted as a stand-alone document so it can be shared with potential investors, and other interested parties. Should they want or need more information, the full plan can be provided upon their request.

Following the executive summary is the *business overview* section, which details exactly what the business does and how it creates value for its customers and society. It also illustrates where the business is in its life, such as in concept stage, operational but not yet profitable, or profitable and seeking investment. The business overview also gives the entrepreneur an opportunity to describe the product and spell out the value proposition for the reader, as well as provide additional information on the competitive advantage that the venture has in the marketplace. This section also lends itself well to outlining the mission, vision, and values of the company. As one of the first sections of the business plan, the business overview should be exciting and engaging to entice the reader to continue reading the remainder of the document.

BOX 6.2 KEY COMPONENTS OF A BUSINESS PLAN

Cover Page

Table of Contents

I. Executive Summary
A two page summary of the business plan

II. Business Overview
A description of the business, product, technology, and the opportunity. It also includes the competitive advantage and present status

III. Industry and Market Overview
A detailed analysis of the industry sector, relevant trends, market size, defined target market, and competitive analysis

IV. Marketing Plan
A description of the 4 Ps of marketing as related to the business model and opportunity

V. Management Team
An overview of the management team and their relevant experience, roles and responsibilities. The board and other advisors should also be included in this section.

VI. Company Structure
An overview of the legal form and organizational structure and hierarchy

VII. Operations Plan
Overview of how the company will run on a day to day basis, e.g. customer service, quality control, facilities, business relationships.

VIII. Risks and Mitigation Strategies
List of current risks and how they will be addressed

IX. Sustainability Plan and Metrics
SROI, Lifecycle Analysis, Carbon Footprint

X. Financial Plan
An outline of capital requirements and requests based on financial projections. Pro forma financial statements and exit strategy should be included.

XI. Appendix
Supporting documents as needed

Source: Barringer, Bruce; Ireland, Duane, *Entrepreneurship: Successfully Launching New Ventures,* 2nd Ed., (c) 2008. Reprinted and Electronically reproduced by permission of Pearson Education, Inc. Upper Saddle River NJ 07458.

Next in the business plan writing process is the *industry and market overview,* which should include a detailed analysis of the market for the good or service being provided by the venture. This helps the entrepreneur and other readers to understand the company's true potential. The analysis should also detail the industry in which the sustainable venture is operating, the industry trends, the overall market, and how much of the market the sustainable venture can capture over time. Of course, this will help derive the financial statements and *pro forma* models that should be included in the financial section of the business plan. A study of the competitive landscape of the industry is also important. Knowing whom the sustainable venture is competing against will help to benchmark success and can help support the value proposition—for example, *we are faster than X, we are better than Y, we are more affordable than Z.*

Having explored the competitive landscape and detailed the competitive advantages that a sustainable venture has over the competition will aid the formation of the next section of the business plan, which is the marketing plan. In the marketing plan the company will need to define its *marketing mix,* which has traditionally been explained using the *Four Ps:* Product, Price, Promotion, and Place.[15]

Product clearly defines the product, be it a good or service, the sustainable venture will provide.

Price is the pricing strategy the company will employ for its good or service.

Promotion is the manner in which the good or service will be shared with the desired audience and what the key messaging is for the sustainable venture and for the goods or services it provides.

Placement is the distribution and channel strategy the company will employ to disseminate the good or service to its customer.

The next part of the plan is the *management team* section. This is arguably one of the most important sections of the plan for a new venture, because investors and others will focus on the person or people launching the venture. The management team section should detail who is involved in the management of the company, their relevant experience, and what their roles and responsibilities will be in the operation of the company. This is also the place to include the members of the board, if one exists, and the advisers. It is important to show who is engaged in the company and in what capacity they are serving the business. Should the venture not have all of the human resources it needs to fulfill the mission of the company, the management team section is also a good place to indicate whom the next key hires will be. No one is expecting the business to have everything it needs, but the plan should spell out what human resources are necessary make the business successful.

Now that the reader knows what the company does and who is on the team, the next section should include is the *company structure* section. This part can be brief, but nonetheless, it should state clearly what the company's legal structure is and why the structure was chosen. If you are pursuing other certifications, such as B Corp status, this should also be included in the company structure portion of the plan. This section should also include an organizational chart that depicts how the chain of command works in the particular venture.

The next portion of the plan should be the *operations plan.* This portion should include how the product or service is going to be delivered to the customer, and how the venture will control for quality in its processes. This section should also detail the how the company will interact with its customers and clients and how the customer support system works. Not to be overlooked are the business partnerships that need to be implemented; these can be extremely important if the entrepreneur is considering collaboration with governmental agencies, non-governmental organizations, or other firms, as many sustainable ventures do.

A sustainable venture plan may require additional components aside from the regular operations including the practices that set the company apart from a traditional commercial enterprise and communicate the actions the sustainable venture is taking to operate according to its values. Outdoor apparel and equipment manufacturer GoLite exemplifies such operational practices. The company has an extensive set of sustainability practices designed to reduce environmental impact and "go lite" on the environment (see Box 6.3). Following is a list of actions to consider adding in the operations plan for you sustainable venture:

- Recycling and waste stream management programs
- Product design standards (cradle-to-cradle design)

GoLite's innovative tactical environmental plan is based on their marketing and operations plan. Notice that their values are present in their plan.

GoLite's stated "Meaning of Life" started with a simple idea. That experiencing nature would be better with less. Less weight, less fuss, less waste … more fun. It's a philosophy that drives their company to make simple, beautiful high performance gear that's light on the planet.

GoLite also has a sustainability focus that includes the following elements:

- *Transparency:* GoLite issues an annual Sustainability Report.
- *Product Impact:* GoLite has made a shift towards Environmentally Preferred Materials (EPMs) and creates products that are lighter, use less material and create less waste.
- *Responsible Production and Fair Trade Labor:* GoLite audits 100% of their production facilities to ensure that their products are made by suppliers in a fair, safe and non-discriminatory manner
- *Product take back Program:* GoLite's innovative "I'm Not Trash" product take back program keeps GoLite products out of the landfill. All GoLite products can be sent back to the company for repair, donation, repurpose, or stored for future recycling.
- *Climate Impact:* GoLite has made the decision to be carbon neutral, and they offset all of their carbon emissions from factory through consumer with NativeEnergy credits.

Source: www.golite.com

- Product take-back programs
- Human resource policies designed for diverse employee groups and employees with children
- Employee Stock Ownership Program (ESOP)
- Travel methods
- Transport of goods
- Supplier relations and accountability
- Health and wellness programs
- Paid volunteer time in the community

- Corporate giving and charitable contributions
- Other items that feed into the company's values and mission

Following the operations plan section is the *risks and mitigation strategies* portion. Readers of a business plan know that there are inherent risks to operating a business. This section provides the opportunity to show that that the entrepreneur has thought through some of the risks and has a strategy to mitigate their potential negative impact on the company. Risks can include everything from unsecured intellectual property, to single source supplier risk, to foreign exchange risk if the company operates across international borders. Showing that one has thought through potential challenges illustrates that the entrepreneur is not going into this blindly and has the ability to overcome the hurdles that may stand in his or her way. In Chapter 7, we will return to the subject of risk and further discuss the importance of various types of risk in the new venture.

A section regarding sustainability metrics may also be included and should detail the measures the company will use to verify the creation of social and/or environmental value. This section should include many of the applicable metrics that we will discuss later in this chapter and the section will show to readers that the entrepreneur is serious about these issues and has a plan in place to monitor and measure performance in this area of the business.

The penultimate section of the business plan is the *financial plan*, where all of the previous sections come together in monetary terms. This section will forecast the business's financial performance, typically through *pro forma* financial statements, which include the Balance Sheet, Income Statement, and Statement of Cash flows. In most cases one makes an educated guess about how the company will perform over time; five years is typical. Because we know that even the best guesses can be wrong, it is advisable to model three scenarios. The first is a low-growth scenario that ideally depicts at least break-even performance. The second should be the most-likely scenario, which hopefully shows the company making a profit. And the third scenario should be the most optimistic scenario. This will give you and your readers an idea of what resources it will take to achieve the company's economic goals, and what might happen if expectations are not met, or hopefully, exceeded. A synopsis of the *pro forma* statements should be included in this section, but the entirety of the statements should appear in the appendices. The financials section should also include plans for funding, including the sources and uses of your funding as well as what investors or lenders will be offered in return for their support.

Finally, the plan should include an appendix of relevant documents; this is the place to put more detailed information in support of the business plan. As mentioned, all of the *pro forma* financial statements should be included in the appendix. It is common for the management team to also include team members' résumés in the appendix as well. Supporting articles, data, and references can also be placed in the appendix.

Although much of the business planning for sustainable ventures is similar to traditional business planning, planning for a sustainable venture requires some added considerations as discussed above. Although it is necessary to incorporate the underlying business approach and prospects, it is often equally important to show passion for the business and enthusiasm for the idea. Thus, the plan can serve as a storytelling tool, narrating the business's genesis and the powerful change it could produce in the world.

LEGAL FORMS OF ORGANIZATION

Establishing a company as a legal entity is one of the first things that an entrepreneur will do as he or she builds a sustainable venture. There are many different options for the legal structure of an organization, and as any great designer knows, and every entrepreneur should also realize, *form follows function.* This old design adage is helpful in the entrepreneurial space because the legal structure of a company will affect certain business dealings and can have lasting legal and economic ramifications for a business. Moreover, some exciting new legal forms of organization, created specifically for the social sector and mission-driven companies, have emerged in the past several years.

Corporate structure is an important decision, and there are a number of legal business entities to choose from, each with its own set of advantages and disadvantages. The following are factors that you will want to consider as you launch your venture:

- Personal liability for the actions of the venture
- Formalities, rules and regulations from governmental agencies
- Attractiveness to investors
- Anonymity of ownership
- Tax-deductible benefits for employees
- Allowance of foreign investors
- Flexibility in management and organization
- Allowance of different classes of stock
- Pass-through of profits and losses to owners via personal tax returns

The choice of legal structure will certainly affect things like investment activity, tax liability, corporate board structure, and company oversight. Although the corporate structure can be changed if necessary, one should find the option that best suits the type of company being created in advance, rather than making time-consuming and potentially costly changes later on. Traditional options for corporate structure, each with its own idiosyncrasies, are *sole proprietorship, partnership, limited liability company, S Corporation,* or *C Corporation.* Seeking legal advice regarding the most advantageous model for a particular sustainable venture is highly recommended.

That said, there are some new and exciting opportunities for sustainable enterprises that have recently begun to take hold within the business community. As we know, some social and sustainable ventures may be willing to sacrifice some level of profitability to achieve their social goals. This can create conflict, particularly in companies with external investors, which are legally bound to maximize shareholder financial wealth. In the most famous example, the board of Ben & Jerry's Ice Cream was compelled to sell the company to Unilever, at least partially because it was required by law to maximize shareholder value. In response to this type of conflict, new legal forms of organization are arising to accommodate socially and environmentally oriented founders and investors:[16, 17]

L3C: The *low-profit, limited-liability company* (L3C) legal structure is now available in a number states in the United States. Like an LLC, it limits investor liability and offers pass through taxation, but enables the enterprise to prioritize social goals over financial ones. A company with the L3C designation has an advantage because it can couple its for-profit efficiencies with less IRS regulations to meet its social and/or environmental goals.

Benefit Corp: The *benefit corporation* is another new corporate legal structure that requires the organization to operate to the public benefit, defined as a material positive benefit to society and the environment. Benefit corporations must have a social or environmental intent and serve the interests of workers, the environment, and community, as well as shareholders. Outdoor clothing company Patagonia was the first company to become a registered benefit corporation in California. Currently seven states in the United States recognize the benefit corporation as a legal form of incorporation. The benefit corporation is not just a U.S.-based concept. The United Kingdom also allows the formation of *community interest companies,* which permit the pursuit of similar missions. Whether these new organizational forms will prove successful remains to be seen, but they are clearly gaining in popularity. At the least, they open up new options for social and environmental entrepreneurs (and their investors) who wish to prioritize social or environmental benefit.

Nonprofit: A nonprofit organization is a legal structure defined by the government that requires the organization to employ its surplus revenue to achieve its mission, rather than distributing the profits to owners. In other words, nonprofits must retain surplus revenues to reinvest in the organization. The surplus can be used to grow the nonprofit's scope, scale, and impact. Nonprofits may be managed by paid staff (such as an executive director) or by a group of volunteers that believe in the mission of the organization. From a sustainable venturing standpoint, this legal form can be beneficial for entities that may need to seek grant funding or that cannot be self-sustained by operational revenues.

The legal structure of a sustainable venture is indeed important, as investors prefer some structures over others, and certain structures can more easily attract capital from various sources. Moreover, the certifications and designations that a sustainable venture seeks can send a strong signal to its market about what the company stands for and how it does business. When starting out, entrepreneurs should explore the options that exist for their venture and determine which will be the most advantageous for their business.

TEAM: GET THE RIGHT PEOPLE IN THE RIGHT PLACES

Building a great team geared toward making the sustainable venture a successful business is challenging but rewarding. It is also one of the most important responsibilities an entrepreneur faces when launching a new business. A venture team is composed of the people who take a business from concept to operational enterprise and beyond: the founding members, employees, investors, board members, and advisers involved in the start-up and growth of the venture. The quality of the venture team is important for a number of reasons. Foremost, of course, are the skills, abilities, and networks that team members bring to the venture. The entrepreneur should consider how such skills complement existing capabilities and endeavor to build a team diverse enough to accomplish the various tasks. In the process of enhancing diversity in expertise, the entrepreneur should consider functional areas including finance, accounting, marketing, operations, engineering, and design. It is also important to try to find people who know the industry in which they are mobilizing resources and have a track record of success.[18] Overall, finding experienced team members is a great way to overcome limitations in the founder's experience or expertise.

The quality of the team is also an important signal to potential investors, customers, and suppliers. A top-notch, experienced, and skilled team adds legitimacy to the enterprise and builds external parties' confidence in the venture. So the entrepreneur should think not only about what skills are needed, but also about how the team signals the prospects of the company. Indeed, a common rule of thumb in investor communities is that they are investing more in the team than they are in the specific entrepreneurial opportunity. Engaging highly reputable and experienced team members, whether founders, employees, or advisors, helps build faith that the organization can succeed. Likewise, to attract and retain a solid team, the entrepreneur should have a reputation of integrity, trust, and commitment to their work and mission. Even a young, relatively inexperienced founder can mobilize a great team through networks and reputation. In fact, a great team may be all he or she has to rely on when first entering the business world.

Creating a venture team takes time, effort, and forethought. Often, the team does not come together at one particular instance, but rather coalesces over time as the venture adds human resources to execute its strategy.[19] In some cases an entrepreneur may rely on uncompensated help from friends or family and may recruit volunteers aligned with their mission and values. This may be an advantage for the sustainable entrepreneur when first starting out, especially if the venture is not fully funded or low on monetary resources. Recruiting individuals who are already on board with the company's mission may make it easier for the entrepreneur to find people willing to forgo compensation to work for a venture in which they believe.

Many sustainable venture teams are brought together through shared networks and networking events for start-ups and entrepreneurs. You will find a growing number of entrepreneurship networking events across the world. Some groups are more formal than others. For example, events created for fundraising purposes may be extremely controlled and monitored. Others may be more like industry "mixers," where people within the same field get together to talk about and hear presentations on new ideas and companies in their area of business. Regardless of the event, one may find that networking at events for entrepreneurs is a great way to meet future partners, advisors, employees, and investors.

One of the first decisions that will be made regarding the sustainable venture team is the founding-member structure. In other words, the initial founder will need to decide if there is just one founding member or a team of founding individuals who will be catalysts for the sustainable enterprise. Although there is nothing wrong with having a solo founder, studies show that 50 to 70 percent of all new businesses are started by teams rather than individuals.[20] It is widely accepted that sustainable venture teams with more than one member have greater talent, ideas, professional experience, networks, and capital to offer. Different points of view can add to the sustainable venture's ability to creatively solve problems and identify paths to success. However, with the benefits of more founding members come potential drawbacks. There can be conflict within teams, especially among those who have not previously worked together. Team dynamics can be challenging to manage, especially in a potentially stressful start-up environment. Developing clear expectations to which all founding members agree can help minimize the potential for trouble later on. Making sure that the founding team is aligned to the mission and values of the company is an important starting point, as this will set the tone for others who join the business at a later point.

After the founding members are specified, attracting employees is key. Of course, there are technical areas of expertise that need to be added. Job advertisements, recruiters, and temporary employment agencies are all good sources for finding employees with the right skills. Temporary agencies are often a good source for the new venture that faces some uncertainty in the magnitude of work necessary. Temporary employment is also a way to test the skills and fit of new employees, because the venture does not have to commit to a long time period.

Entrepreneurs can easily get an idea of salaries for various types of employees through online salary-benchmarking websites. The entrepreneur may also wish to remunerate employees through a combination of salary and stock ownership plans (such as a stock option plan). Such plans may allow the company to pay a lower salary than market rates, as the lower salary is offset by the potential future value of equity ownership.

In a sustainable enterprise, employees should also be committed to the company mission and values. Values may be a major source of competitive advantage, and hiring employees aligned with those values is critical. In addition, the sustainable venture's mission and values may be helpful in recruiting new employees because many people will prioritize working for a company whose mission they support. Yvon Chouinard, founder of Patagonia, seeks out employees who are passionate about the company and its products. Indeed, their interests in outdoor activities mean more to Patagonia than having certain skill sets. Chouinard states, "Finding a dyed-in-the-wool businessperson to take up climbing or river running is a lot more difficult than teaching a person with a ready passion for the outdoors to do a job."[21]

The entrepreneur of a sustainable venture must inspire passion in employees who are hired into the company, as they will be the early evangelists for the company. As Chouinard explains, they should be on board with the company's mission and practices.

Another important aspect of building a venture team is the group of advisors, consultants, and directors who assist the company. The choice of advisors and directors is particularly important because they can add legitimacy, connections, and important expertise to the venture. In choosing these individuals, the entrepreneur should aim high and try to attract experienced and seasoned experts, counselors, entrepreneurs, and/or industry professionals. Advisors, directors, and consultants can also complement the team without requiring full-time salaries and benefits. The entrepreneur should therefore use these positions strategically, understanding that they provide another means of building the team even with scarce resources.

To be certain, selecting and attracting a new venture team is a critical process for the entrepreneur, and building good human resources requires thought and consideration of many elements. But the sustainable entrepreneur can use enthusiasm for a great business idea to attract top quality talent and individuals, and the resulting team can serve as a foundation for its success.

METRICS: MEASURE SUCCESS AND PERFORMANCE IN A SUSTAINABLE VENTURE

The world of sustainable venturing is filled with exciting ideas and business concepts that can have a powerful impact on the world. When it comes time to bring those ideas into reality, the entrepreneur, donors, and investors will need to know if the venture is working. Developing metrics of success helps the entrepreneur to understand if the venture is achieving its goals.

The old business cliché "What gets measured, gets managed" carries a lot of weight in any venture. But in a sustainable venture, metrics may be even more important because the organization's goals may transcend financial success. In addition, there are some important and meaningful metrics that go above and beyond the traditional balance sheet, income statement, and cash flow statement. Without a doubt, the way that a sustainable venture measures its internal performance and external outcomes is important to the company's viability, scalability, and credibility.

The first step in developing a system of metrics and performance measurement is to understand basic organizational goals. In other words, there needs to be some definition of a good outcome. Defining success can be a tricky task for entrepreneurs because the motivations for launching a sustainable venture can be varied. Entrepreneurs might launch a business to make a lifestyle change, provide for their family, challenge themselves, impact their community, make a lot of money, or change the world.[22] But if they cannot state clearly and succinctly what they are trying to do, then it will be challenging to create systems and mechanisms to monitor progress and forward momentum. On the flip side, if the entrepreneur can communicate what he or she has set out to do, then measurement systems can be constructed to help discover whether the entrepreneur is indeed accomplishing those goals. This, in turn, helps to identify the activities that contribute to the success of the company (and those that do not) and to focus efforts on constantly improving performance.[23]

By understanding exactly what the sustainable venture is trying to accomplish, one can begin to *track, measure, and improve* it. Keeping the end in mind can help the sustainable entrepreneur resist getting bogged down in measuring tasks or actions rather than measuring the outcomes or results. The entrepreneur should start by examining the cause-and-effect relationship between certain activities that the company and its team undertake to create value, as well as the outcomes that result. The activities that drive results can then be systematically modified to increase the desired outcomes.[24] There are indeed some activities and results that are going to be more easily measured than others, so it will be important to focus on the most important elements of the work and its results. The entrepreneur will also want to make sure that the measurement system designed is not too cumbersome, expensive, or time-consuming. Having a coherent system of measurement makes it easier for customers, suppliers, partners, and investors to compare and assess. Indeed, many companies have been tracking social and environmental data for years. However, it is becoming increasingly important to share this information publically, as the demand for corporate transparency increases.

There are many tools that a company can employ to evaluate social and environmental performance. An increasingly popular tool is the *B Corp assessment* and certification tool. There are over 560 (and growing) certified B Corp in the United States representing over sixty industry sectors and $3.35 billion in revenues. Any company, regardless of legal form, can become a certified B Corp (see Figure 6.2). While it is sometimes confused with a benefit corporation, a B Corp is not a form of legal incorporation, it is a certification standard available to companies that meet specific operational standards. The metrics necessary to achieve B Corp certification range from workforce issues, to environmental stewardship, to value-chain accountability and community involvement.

FIGURE 6.2   B Corp Declaration of Interdependence

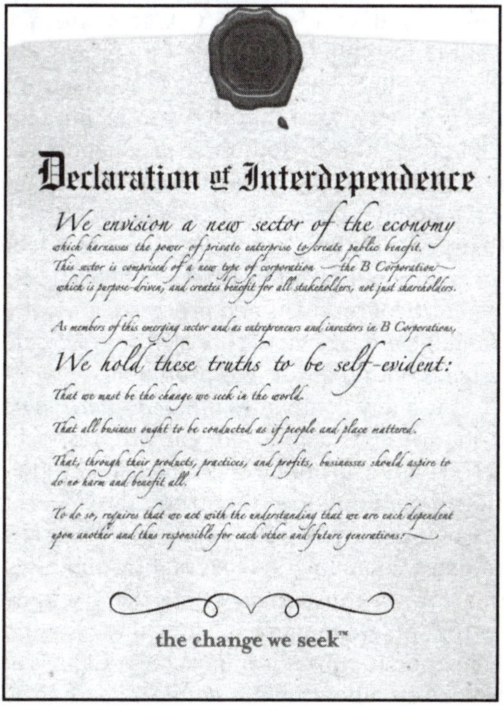

Declaration of Interdependence

We envision a new sector of the economy
which harnesses the power of private enterprise to create public benefit.
This sector is comprised of a new type of corporation — the B Corporation —
which is purpose-driven, and creates benefit for all stakeholders, not just shareholders.

As members of this emerging sector and as entrepreneurs and investors in B Corporations,

We hold these truths to be self-evident:

That we must be the change we seek in the world.

That all business ought to be conducted as if people and place mattered.

That, through their products, practices, and profits, businesses should aspire to
do no harm and benefit all.

To do so, requires that we act with the understanding that we are each dependent
upon another and thus responsible for each other and future generations.

the change we seek™

Source: "Declaration of Interdependence," http://www.bcorporation.net/what-are-b-corps/the-b-corp-declaration, accessed January 24, 2013

The B Corp assessment tool measures a myriad of company activities in categories such as governance, workers, community, and environment.[25] The assessment tool is free and can be used by any company; it is a simple and affordable way to see how one's sustainable venture performs in the social and environmental space in a broad sense.

There are also more specific tools that a sustainable venture can use to measure its performance in the environmental space, especially in terms of greenhouse gas emissions and the environmental impact of its product or service. *Life cycle analysis* (LCA) is a technique to assess the environmental aspects and potential impacts associated with a product, process, or service by

- compiling an inventory of relevant energy and material inputs and environmental releases,
- evaluating the potential environmental impacts associated with identified inputs and releases, and
- interpreting the results to help make more informed decisions.[26]

The United States Environmental Protection Agency (EPA) promotes the use of LCA to allow companies to make informed choices through meaningful understanding of the human health and environmental impacts of products, processes, and activities. The EPA has published detailed information about how a company should conduct a formal LCA; this information can be found both in print and online through the agency. The EPA website is http://www. epa.gov/nrmrl/std/lca/lca.html. The LCA tool supports growing interest in the thoughtful design of products, such that they are high quality, safe, and minimize environmental impacts throughout their production, use, and disposal.[27]

The idea of creating products with their end of life in mind has been articulated by William McDonough's *cradle-to-cradle* philosophy. The cradle-to-cradle concept dictates that products and processes be so intelligently designed that they create positive environmental effects and a beneficial ecological footprint.[28] Although the vast majority of products and processes are not yet designed in this manner, many sustainable entrepreneurs are striving to create a future in which cradle-to-cradle design is both realistic and profitable.

In addition to LCA, many companies are using *carbon accounting* as a way of measuring their impact on the environment with respect to the emission of greenhouse gasses (GHGs). Carbon accounting refers to the process of measuring the amount of carbon dioxide (or carbon dioxide equivalents of other GHGs) released by a company. Understanding GHG emissions is a rapidly growing function in many companies. As legislation and regulations around the globe are mandating carbon constraints within the economy, GHG emissions can pose a liability for some companies. Thus, understanding the company's GHG emissions and carbon footprint is important in today's economy. Although many large corporations are undertaking significant carbon accounting projects, smaller firms are not left out of the picture. New Belgium Brewing released a study evaluating the carbon footprint of one six-pack of Fat Tire beer. The assessment took into consideration the acquisition and transport of raw materials, brewing operations, business travel, employee commuting, transport and storage during distribution and retail, and use and disposal of waste.[29] The study found that over 62 percent of the GHG emissions resulted from electricity used for refrigeration at retail and the production and transportation of glass and malt. This was no small project, but only by understanding its carbon footprint could New Belgium Brewing take measurable steps to improve.

A young sustainable venture may not have the resources to conduct a full LCA or carbon accounting program at the outset. However, another tool in the sustainable entrepreneur's tool bag is *social return on investment* (SROI) analysis. A traditional *economic return on investment* (ROI) analysis is a commonly used financial measure for evaluating the economic consequences of monetary investments. As the name implies, the ROI model predicts the potential financial reward of making an investment in certain activities. The SROI approach takes this basic framework and uses it to create a monetary representation of the social, economic, and environmental outcomes created by activities that do not typically have an evident market value.

SROI can be a powerful tool for the sustainable entrepreneur, as investors may be seeking to place their capital in a company that is creating economic benefit and social/environmental benefit. An accurate assessment and calculation of positive societal and environmental outcomes can be a critical influencing factor in a potential funders' decision process. Moreover, SROI can help tell the whole story of the sustainable venture and augment the economic story. Of course, the SROI measures will vary greatly between sustainable ventures. A social return for a company that builds private schools in underdeveloped nations will indeed look different than a company that builds clean burning biomass stoves to reduce indoor air pollution.

In addition to using these tools, sustainable entrepreneurs might want to consider unintended negative consequences of their organizations' actions, such as the extent to which they have altered a regional culture. For example, one of the unintended consequences of Grameen Bank's microfinancing enterprise was an increase in domestic violence. This appeared to be a function of its female-only lending policy. Although the social and economic value created from the operation has been extraordinary, there were still some side effects of the company's actions. Recognizing that societal interventions can create unintended consequences is a good start to considering consequences of one's own venture.

In today's globalized world, sustainable entrepreneurs might also consider how different cultural values or norms might impact how others perceive of what they prioritize and do. Inherent philosophical, scientific, and economic tradeoffs often exist in even the most basic issues. Is it "better" to provide fresh, local, natural, and organic food or to produce inexpensive food for the poor? Is a venture in expensive solar photovoltaic panels superior to a new means of extracting natural gas? Is bringing new technology to indigenous cultures an opportunity for economic development or the destruction of a sustainable culture? While people might disagree on any of these examples, it nevertheless requires a judgment call that can create challenges for the sustainable entrepreneur. In the end, such choices are left to the social entrepreneur, but perhaps subject to judgment of external parties who may impact the venture's success, or perception thereof.

Summary

Managing and implementing a sustainable venture can be extremely challenging yet amazingly rewarding for the entrepreneur. We know that the sustainable venture is set apart from a traditional venture, and that a sustainable venture is sometimes driven by a guiding mission and core set of values that goes beyond creating shareholder value. In this chapter we have discussed six primary elements of building a sustainable venture: mission, values, plan, legal structure, team, and metrics. Each of these elements is critical to the success of the venture and is nuanced for the sustainable venture application. The mission and values set the stage for the venture and guide operational strategies and performance metrics. The team that serves a sustainable venture should align with the mission and values and as such serve as evangelists for the company and its goals. With a strong mission, the company's culture can also serve as a competitive advantage for finding and keeping talented individuals. Like traditional start-ups, the sustainable venture must plan its success and how it will be achieved. However, there are additional considerations the sustainable venture must include in its business plan, such as its commitment to social justice and or environmental stewardship and its metrics for nonfinancial performance (such as SROI, carbon accounting, or LCA). Sustainable ventures can also consider unique legal structures. Benefit corporations, nonprofits, or L3Cs can help signal to the market what the company believes and how it acts in the business world. These innovative business structures also allow companies to pursue goals other than increasing shareholder value and are a powerful tool for networking, fundraising, and marketing. Launching a sustainable venture can be challenging, but with proper forethought and planning, one can increase his or her odds of succeeding at business and creating positive impact.

Key Learnings

1. The six key elements of managing and building a sustainable venture are mission, values, plan, legal form, team, and metrics.
2. A *mission* is a concise understanding or statement about why the company exists. In a sustainable venture, the mission tends to incorporate its social and or environmental purpose. A written mission statement can be a powerful tool for showing customers, employees, the community, investors, and other businesses what a sustainable venture is all about.
3. *Values* are the guiding principles and philosophies that drive the company's conduct, decision-making, and its relationships with external stakeholders.
4. The process of *planning* is a critical step in launching a sustainable venture. A *business plan* is a formal written document detailing specific elements of the business and how they will be implemented to achieve the company's goals. A sustainable venture sets itself apart by incorporating plans and actions tied to its values and mission.
5. One of the first things an entrepreneur will do in launching a venture is select the legal form of ownership. Traditional legal forms include sole proprietorship, partnership, LLC, S Corp, C Corp, and Non-Profit.
6. New legal forms are taking root in the business community. These include the *benefit corporation,* and the *L3C.* The benefit corporation and L3C may have specific advantages for social and sustainable enterprises.
7. Creating the management team is arguably one of the most important elements in launching a sustainable venture. A *venture team* is the group of people who take a business from concept to an operational enterprise. The team is comprised of the founding members, key employees, investors, directors, and advisers involved in the growth of the venture. The team's cultural fit and alignment with the mission and values are important for a sustainable venture. The venture's mission and values can be a key asset in recruiting passionate and qualified people to the company.

8. Defining success can be a tricky but invaluable exercise for a sustainable entrepreneur. Knowing exactly what the company wants to achieve is imperative to developing *metrics* that track success. Some company actions can have unintended consequences that the company will need to measure and address. Examples of measurement systems used by some sustainable ventures are the *B Corp assessment, life cycle analysis (LCA), carbon accounting, and social return on investment (SROI).*

Endnotes

1. "How To Write Your Mission Statement: Summing Up Your Business's Mission Helps You Focus On the Steps You Need to Take to Succeed: Here's How To Create A Mission Statement That's Uniquely Yours," *Entrepreneur Magazine,* October, 2003.
2. "Social Mission, Greyston Bakery, http://www.greystonbakery.com/social-mission/, accessed January 24, 2013.
3. "Guiding Principles," Greyston Bakery, http://www.greystonbakery.com/wp-content/uploads/pdf/greyston-bakery-guiding-principles.pdf, accessed January 24, 2013.
4. "Values," *Business Dictionary,* http://www.businessdictionary.com/definition/values. html, accessed January 24, 2013.
5. "Our Story," New Belgium Brewing, http://www.newbelgium.com/culture/our-story. aspx, accessed January 24, 2013.
6. Dwight D. Eisenhower, Speech to the National Defense Executive Reserve Conference in Washington, DC (November 14, 1957), in *Public Papers of the Presidents of the United States, Dwight D. Eisenhower, 1957*, National Archives and Records Service, Government Printing Office, p. 818.
7. Getting to Scale: Growing Your Business Without Selling Out. Bamberg, J. Berrett-KoehlerPublishers, Inc. San Francisco, CA. 2006
8. Small Giants: Companies that choose to be great instead of big. Burlingham, B. Penguin Group (USA) Inc. New York, NY. 2005
9. Getting to Scale: Growing Your Business Without Selling Out. Bamberg, J. Berrett-KoehlerPublishers, Inc. San Francisco, CA. 2006
10. Johnson, M. W., Christensen, C. M., & Kagermann, H. (2008). Reinventing your business model. *Harvard business review*, 86(12), 57–68.
11. Entrepreneurship: Successfully Launching New Ventures. Barringer, B., Ireland, D. Pearson Education, Inc. Upper Saddle River, New Jersey. 2008
12. Entrepreneurship: Successfully Launching New Ventures. Barringer, B., Ireland, D. Pearson Education, Inc. Upper Saddle River, New Jersey. 2008
13. Ibid.
14. Ibid.
15. "Sustainability at GoLite," GoLite, http://www.golite.com/Info/Meaning-Of-Lite/ Sustainability.aspx?f=1, accessed January 23, 2013.
16. K. Westaway, "New Legal Structures for "Social Entrepreneurs," *Wall Street Journal*, December 12, 2011.
17. "B Corps: Firms with Benefits: A New Sort of Caring, Sharing Company Gathers Momentum," *The Economist,* January 7, 2012, available at http://www.economist. com/node/21542432/print, accessed January 24, 2013.
18. J. Wei-skillern, J. Austin, H. Leonard, and H. Stevenson, *Entrepreneurship in the Social Sector* (Thousand Oaks, CA: Sage Publications, 2007).

19. B. Barringer and D. Ireland, *Entrepreneurship: Successfully Launching New Ventures* (Upper Saddle River, NJ: Pearson, 2008)
20. M. Gruber and J. Henkel, "New Ventures Based on Open Innovation- An Empirical Analysis of Start-up Firms in Embedded Linux," *International Journal of Technology Management* 33 (2006): 356–372
21. Y. Choinard, *Let My People Go Surfing: The Education of a Reluctant Businessman* (New York: Penguin, 2006), p. 168
22. J. Bamberg, *Getting to Scale: Growing Your Business Without Selling Out* San Francisco: Berrett-KoehlerPublishers, 2006.
23. Wei-skillern, Austin, Leonard, and Stevenson, *Entrepreneurship in the Social Sector.*
24. Ibid.
25. "How to Become a B Corp," http://www.bcorporation.net/become-a-b-corp/how-to-become-a-b-corp, accessed January 24, 2013.
26. "Life Cycle Assessment (LCA)," United States Environmental Protection Agency, http://www.epa.gov/nrmrl/std/lca/lca.html, accessed July 2012.
27. W. McDonough, and M. Broungart, *Cradle to Cradle: Remaking the Things We Make* New York: North Point Press, 2002).
28. Corporate Environmental Strategy Volume 9, Issue 3, August 2002, Pages 251–258
29. "The Carbon Footprint of Fat Tire® Amber Ale," The Climate Conservancy, 2008, available online at http://www.newbelgium.com/Files/the-carbon-footprint-of-fat-tire-amber-ale-2008-public-dist-rfs.pdf, accessed January 24, 2013.

CHAPTER 7

FINANCING THE SUSTAINABLE VENTURE

INTRODUCTION

Like most ventures, sustainable ventures typically need funding to start and grow. In the early stages of a venture, small amounts may be required for legal incorporation, prototype development, and the purchase of equipment and materials. Some new ventures require large sums for technology development, salaries, or other needs. As a company grows, it may require even greater funds for expansion and working capital to fund the lag between production and cash flows. Sustainable entrepreneurs need to understand current, as well as future financing needs, and to plan accordingly. Although many of the sources, strategies, and processes of venture funding are the same for sustainable ventures as for any other, sustainable ventures also have some unique financing approaches and opportunities. Financing the sustainable venture may be easier when financiers are excited about the positive social or environmental impact of the venture. Although this is not always the case, the potential for positive impact may allow the entrepreneur to attract sources of capital that would not otherwise be available.

We first discuss the basic types and sources of venture funding. We then discuss two basic questions entrepreneurs should ask before seeking financing for their firms. We next move to a discussion of the relationship between valuation and risk, as these are critical concepts to the entrepreneur interested in attracting equity investments. We conclude with a discussion of some of the unique sources of financing available to the sustainable venture.

TYPES OF VENTURE FUNDING

The primary types of funding for new ventures include bootstrapping, financing from cash flow, financing from debt, and financing from equity. *Bootstrapping* refers to the various ways a venture can reduce costs, find innovative ways to avoid expenditures, or use other people's resources to accomplish their goals. The goal of bootstrapping is to reduce, delay, or eliminate the need for external funding in a new venture. The classic example is the garage venture, in which founders use their garage to start the business at low cost. Hewlett-Packard, one of the early technology pioneers, was founded in a garage in Palo Alto, California.[1]

Another approach is to convince service providers (such as lawyers or accountants) or advisors to offer their time or resources to the venture for little or no cash outflow. Often, such providers are motivated by the prospect of future business with the venture, but they may also be excited by the venture or willing to help as a service to the community. Such individuals may be motivated by the prospect of doing something new or of helping a student entrepreneur start a business. Alumni of your school may be particularly amenable to assisting new entrepreneurs. In other cases, these individuals may provide services in exchange for a small equity position in a budding company. Sustainable ventures may be particularly exciting to some of these resource providers, as such ventures offer them the opportunity to engage in a business that can change the world for the better.

Other approaches to bootstrapping include leasing equipment instead of purchasing, buying used equipment instead of new, and using social media marketing instead of traditional advertising. Opportunities for spreading the word about a sustainable venture through public relations efforts also abound. Ventures who contribute to the social good or environmental preservation tend to be particularly attractive to media outlets looking for a good human interest or business story. You should not be afraid to send out news releases about your company and its social or environmental goals. Many media outlets enjoy sharing stories about new concepts and companies, so they may run a story or article on you for free. Free media coverage can get a small firm far in terms of exposure, and legitimacy.

Customers and suppliers may be another way to bootstrap your business. If an entrepreneur can demonstrate substantial potential for a business, suppliers may provide advice or equipment to help the venture get going, likely on the assumption that it will become a future customer. In other cases, suppliers and ventures engage in joint research projects to develop prototypes and new products. Buyers may also be motivated to help ventures get started, as doing so may provide them with a future source of a superior or lower-cost product.

Once a venture gets going and achieves profitability, it may be able to fund its growth through the *cash flow* derived from the business. In some ways, this is ideal. It is more feasible to fund a business from cash flow when the business has high profit margins or low costs of expansion. Both bootstrapping and financing from earnings offer the benefit of avoiding debt or selling equity to other investors. Indeed, many experts argue that the best approach to fundraising is to minimize external capital needs at the start of the business, because founders typically have to sell a significant percentage of the company's stock in its early stages to raise a substantial amount of cash. Thus, the longer a venture can hold out before selling equity, the more likely the founder can retain a larger portion of the company's stock. Of course, this is not always true. When speed to market is important for success, it is sometimes imperative to move as quickly as possible and to immediately raise the capital necessary to get to market and expand quickly. In other cases, the costs of starting or expanding a venture are just too high to fund through bootstrapping or cash flow.

Ventures may also take on *debt* to start or grow their ventures. Debt has the advantage of being non dilutive, in that it does not require the founder to sell a portion of the company for capital. Debt holders also do not typically play a direct role in the management of the company, leaving the founder freer to determine strategy and operations. But debt is difficult to acquire at start-up, unless the company or individual has collateral to offer. Debt also typically requires monthly payments of principal and interest, so it reduces the ongoing cash flow position of the company. If payments are not made, the lender may force the company into bankruptcy and seize its assets in order in order to recover its loan. Founders may take on personal loans (such as a second mortgage on a home) to finance a new venture, or the business itself may find a commercial loan based on inventory, accounts receivable, or other hard assets. In the case of bankruptcy, debt holders typically have preference in the remaining assets, meaning that they get paid back prior to any capital being distributed to the owners of the business.

Because debt is difficult to obtain in a new venture, most entrepreneurs in need of capital look for *equity* investors, who provide money in return for a percentage of ownership in the venture. Equity investors may be looking to acquire a percentage of the ongoing profits from the venture, but they are more often looking for a return from an increase in the value of the stock. Equity capital offers a number of advantages to the budding entrepreneur. First, it provides capital without the need for regular payments, until the company achieves profitability or is in a position to pay dividends. Second, equity investors may bring skills, networks, and other resources into the venture, and they have a vested interest in the company that motivates them to help. Sophisticated equity investors understand the high level of risk associated with new ventures and therefore typically expect a high rate of return.

Entrepreneurs should also understand that many equity investors are looking to liquidate their interests within a relatively short period. In other words, they typically want to sell their stock at a return within a few years of their investment. Venture investors may also require a large percentage of the company in return for their funding. This causes dilution of the founder's stock position and may eventually lead to the point where investors gain control of the company through voting rights and/or board positions. This fact may put the founder's leadership at risk, since investors may take action to protect their investment and preserve the value of their stock. This may result in the founder being asked to step down from the role of chief executive and being replaced by professional management. This is not necessarily a bad development and may be in the interest of the founder, who shares in the financial success of the company.

Equity investment may come from a variety of sources including friends and family, angel investors, venture capitalists, or strategic investors. Many ventures start with investments by the founders' *friends or family*. Of course, taking money from friends and family can be fraught with difficulty, but you may find that some are most willing to help with your entrepreneurial endeavors. Nonetheless, one should be careful not to ask for investments that one's friends and family cannot afford to lose. *Angel investors* are individuals or small groups of investors who have sufficient net worth to engage in new venture investment on a regular basis. They may be motivated by the excitement the entrepreneur demonstrates and the financial or social/environmental potential of the new venture. Angels vary substantially in their level of engagement with a venture, but some only invest when they can play an active role in the company. For that reason, it is wise to look for angel investors who are aligned with the mission of the company. Indeed, proper choice of an angel investor helps insure that future decisions will match the company's core values and beliefs.

Venture capitalists are professional investors who manage funds with the specific purpose of investing in high-potential ventures. They typically operate funds of capital provided by various personal or institutional investors (i.e., pension funds) and identify and invest in ventures with the potential to provide substantial returns. Venture capitalists are typically skilled in the venture development process and bring a variety of resources (in addition to capital) to the table. They expect high rates of return to cover the risks associated with new ventures and often play an active role in the company through positions on the board of directors and other means. There are substantive benefits to attracting venture capital investors, including skills and expertise in venture development and/or in the industry in which you plan to operate. They often have networks of individuals that they can tap to help in the development of a venture. These networks can include experts in legal issues, intellectual property, technology, and markets. Venture capitalists also bring legitimacy to the budding venture and increase confidence from important constituencies, such as customers or suppliers. They may also link to additional sources of funding and help attract other investors. But there can be significant disadvantages in seeking funding from venture capitalists. They are typically skilled negotiators, and you should expect them to bargain and to include terms and preferences that minimize their risk. They may also push for control of the company in order to protect their investment.

Strategic investors are corporations with a strategic interest in the new venture. They typically operate in the same or a related industry as the venture, and want to gain access to knowledge, capabilities, or markets. Strategic investors can be an attractive option for new ventures, as they bring substantive capabilities, in addition to their capital. Many corporations invest through dedicated venture investments groups that exist within their organizations. If the venture succeeds, strategic investors may show an interest in purchasing the entirety of the company and integrating it into their existing business.

FUNDING STRATEGY

Setting out a funding strategy is critical to the sustainable venture. The nature of a funding strategy depends on a number of considerations, and entrepreneurs should ask some critical questions before beginning the process of fundraising. The first, and perhaps most important, question revolves around the personal goals of the founder(s). But entrepreneurs must also consider the financial needs of the venture, given these goals, and the nature of the venture itself.

Question #1: What are my goals?

Entrepreneurs start ventures for a variety of personal reasons, and the nature of the founder's goals determine the type and amount of financing the organization should seek. Some entrepreneurs want to start small businesses that support their family and/or lifestyle. Others start with the intention to found a growth-oriented business with a focus on generating substantial economic returns. Often this involves a plan to sell the business once it reaches a scale large enough to attract a buyer who is willing to pay a substantial sum for the business. In the sustainable venture, financial goals may be secondary to the social or environmental impact the venture hopes to achieve. At the most basic level, the determination of personal goals in venture formation determines the type of financing the venture should seek. In short, funding strategy needs to be aligned with the personal goals of the founders and the venture itself.

Founders wishing to start a small business may want to avoid large equity investments in order to maintain personal control of the business. This is because investors with primarily financial goals may push the company toward higher growth than what is desired by the company or founder. This is particularly true of venture capital investors, as well as some angel investors who often want their investment to be liquid within a period of three to five years. Entrepreneurs wishing to maintain control, keep the business small, or keep growth to a more manageable level are probably best served by seeking funding from friends and family, starting with debt instruments, or avoiding the need for external funding through bootstrapping.

Founders with growth aspirations and a good business model may have the opportunity to access a larger pool of venture investors. Equity investors, like venture capitalists and sophisticated angels, invest in businesses with the potential for high growth and financial returns. Such investors understand the riskiness of new ventures but also the potential return available if the venture succeeds. In order to attract such venture investors, the venture team must show a business model with the potential for large returns in order to accommodate the level of risk venture investors bear when in financing the company.

Founders who place a high priority on social and environmental impact are in a unique position when it comes to seeking investors. Their primary target for funding should be investors who focus on both financial returns and social and environmental impact. Fortunately, the last decade has seen a substantial increase in the numbers of investors who seek to balance impact with financial gain. These *impact investors* may expect competitive returns, but they are at least understanding of multiple priorities, and value a diversity of goals and outcomes. Entrepreneurs who operate nonprofit or hybrid organizations may also be able to access donations or project-based funding from charitable organizations. Increasingly, charitable organizations are focusing their donations on enterprise-based models wherein the donations contribute to a financially sustainable organization or business model that solves a social or environmental problem. We'll further discuss some of the unique sources of financing for the sustainable venture later in this chapter.

Regardless, the most important point is that entrepreneurs should understand their personal and business goals before determining their approach to funding, because their choice may have substantial long-term implications for the outcomes of their ventures. Entrepreneurs who understand their goals and how they align with the goals of their funders will be in a much better position to achieve their aims.

Question #2: How much funding do I need, and when do I need it?

Ventures also vary greatly in the amount of funding needed to start and grow. Some ventures require very little funding and can be developed with minimal capital. Others require little capital at the start, but then require larger amounts to meet increasing market demand and revenue growth. Still others, such as some technology ventures, require years of capital investment before even getting to a marketable product or breakeven cash flow. Entrepreneurs must understand the magnitude and timing of their cash flow needs and develop a plan of funding accordingly.

This is typically done through the development of financial statements in which assumptions are used to forecast revenues and expenditures. Financial forecasts serve as the foundation for setting a fundraising strategy because cash needs at various points in time are understood, or at least estimated. Such forecasts also provide a foundation from which investors can gauge the worth of the business, because the financial forecasts are indicative of the potential cash flows that might result in the future.

Good financial planning is critical for a number of reasons. First, it helps avoid surprises that can cause a company to fail. Second, good financials with clear assumptions signal that the company understands its needs and financial position. Third, financial planning serves as a benchmark from which the company can operate. Deviations from the plan may be noted and adjustments made as the situation changes over time. In addition, new information may be entered into the *pro forma* statements and provide new estimates for the company's fundraising strategy. Finally, once financial statements are created, they can be modified to analyze various *what if* scenarios. In other words, they can be used to examine the outcome of different assumptions. The process of examining the effects of different assumptions (such as lower or higher revenues) on financial outcomes using a financial model is typically referred to as *sensitivity analysis*. Sensitivity analysis is valuable because entrepreneurs and investors want to know what happens when things go worse, or better, than planned.

The rate at which a company spends its cash reserves is typically referred to as the *burn rate*. The burn rate denotes how much cash is being used in a period of time and is usually expressed on a per month basis. Thus, a company with a burn rate of $10,000 is using up $10,000 of cash per month. If the company has $100,000 in the bank due to investments or other sources, it can survive ten months at the current burn rate before it needs an additional influx of capital. The time the company has until it runs out of cash is typically referred to as the *runway*. The length of the runway (usually expressed in months) is critical because it signals how soon the company will need to get to greater levels of revenue, reduce costs, or raise additional capital.

VALUATION AND RISK

Valuation is the process of determining what a company is worth. Valuation is important because it is necessary, or at least implied, in the process of selling equity. If equity investors want to invest capital in your business, what they get in return is stock (a portion of the ownership in your company). An entrepreneur sells stock in his or her company and needs to determine the price at which to offer stock to investors. In the end, the price of the stock is determined by what investors are willing to pay for it, but the process of valuation helps the entrepreneur to arrive at a meaningful estimate and benchmark for negotiation. Typically, founders want to sell their stock at a higher price, while investors seek a lower one.

Valuation can be done in a number of ways. The two most prominent are asset valuations and net present value valuations. Asset valuations calculate the worth of the company by summing the value of the tangible and intangible assets in the company. The tangible, or hard, assets are things like property and equipment. Intangible, or soft, assets include the value of company relationships with suppliers, brand name, human resources, and a host of other capabilities that help the company succeed. As you might expect, putting a dollar figure on such intangible assets is difficult and subjective, particularly in a new venture. As a result, many investors look at net present value calculations to begin negotiations on stock price.

Theoretically, the financial value of a company is equal to the net present value of future cash flows. In other words, the company's worth is related to the level of cash flows it is predicted to receive in the future. The best estimate of future cash flows is calculated in financial forecasts, discussed earlier. Once these numbers are known, it is relatively simple to calculate the net present value of those cash flows using a standard formula available from finance texts or on

FIGURE 7.1 The Relationship Between Risk and Valuation in a Venture

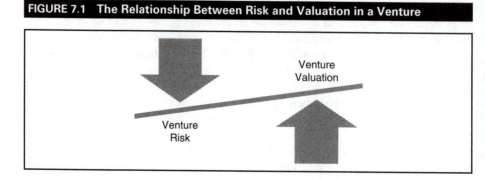

the Internet. Net present value calculations require three basic inputs: forecasted cash flows, the timing of those cash flows, and the discount rate.

The discount rate reflects the fact that most people prefer to have money today, rather than tomorrow. Thus, cash flow in the present is worth more than the same cash flow at some point in the future. But the discount rate also reflects risk. In this case, it reflects the risk that a venture may not achieve its cash flow goals. We all know that failure rates for new ventures are high, so investors want a high expected-rate of return to account for that risk. Thus, discount rates applied in the valuation of new ventures tend to be higher than one might expect. In early stage ventures, for example, discount rates can be as high or higher than 30 percent. Typically, the earlier the stage of the company, the higher is the level of risk. And the higher the perceived risk, the higher is the discount rate that will be applied, and the lower a company's valuation. In short, this means that if a venture is perceived as risky, the entrepreneur will be selling stock to investors at a lower price, all other things equal (See Figure 7.1).

Thus, one of an entrepreneur's top priorities is to reduce the riskiness of the venture. How to accomplish this depends on the nature of the business, but it is instructive to think about the four components of risk that investors consider. (See Figure 7.2)

1. *Market Risk.* Market risk is the uncertainty around whether customers will buy a product or service, and whether they will buy it in the quantity and price forecasted. It seems like market risk is always present, but entrepreneurs can reduce market risk through their actions, even before they have a final product. Market research may help to show customer interest, and a customer letter of support may help as well. But nothing helps prove the point better than actual sales.

2. *Execution Risk.* Starting a business is a complex task involving a multitude of skills and actions. Execution risk refers to the possibility that one will not be able to accomplish the tasks necessary to build the company. It is possible to make many mistakes in hiring, management, planning, organization, or many other areas. Investors will want to know that the entrepreneur and

FIGURE 7.2   Four Components of Risk in New Ventures

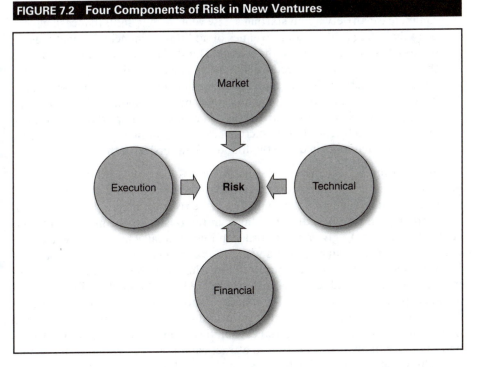

the team can successfully execute their plan. Prior industry, entrepreneurial, or other experience is most helpful in proving one's abilities to investors. But adding top-notch individuals to the team can also speak volumes.

3. *Technical Risk.* Many new ventures start with a new technology or product. Often, those technologies or products are unproven, and/or require development. Technical risk accounts for the possibility that the technology or product may not work. Investors often understand that new ventures face technical risk, but the entrepreneur can demonstrate that the risks are lower in several ways. The development of a prototype of the product, even if it is a simple version, can help show that it will work. One can also use third parties, such as engineering labs, to help validate the viability of your approach. And of course, a completed and marketable product is the best demonstration of minimized technical risk.

4. *Financial Risk.* Many businesses have failed because they ran out of cash or squandered their cash resources. Some have even failed because their finances were mismanaged or because a member of the company embezzled funds. Financial risk reflects the possibility that a company will fail to prosper because it runs out of cash or has insufficient financial resources to expand. It is difficult to prove to investors that an entrepreneur can effectively manage his or her finances. And it is even more difficult to know whether that entrepreneur will be able to raise more cash when the time

comes, even if he or she has achieved results in other areas. Financial risk can increase anxiety about starting a new venture, and faith that cash will be in the offing (either from revenues or additional financing) sometimes seems a fundamental part of the pursuit. But that does not mean that one should not plan for cash needs. Quite the opposite, good entrepreneurs understand cash needs over time and plan for contingencies (such as longer lead times in product development or poor market response) that can effect a company's cash position and viability. Perhaps most importantly, ventures are well served by avoiding cash crunches that allow new investors to negotiate terms that heavily dilute the founders' ownership in the company.

The relationship between risk and valuation is absolutely critical in any venture because the earlier one needs external funding, the more likely one will to have to sell a larger percentage of the company, as the risks are higher. In other words, the more capital required at early stages in the business, the more equity the company will have to give away in order to raise capital. Thus, the key to maintaining one's position in the company may be to minimize the need for financing in early stages. In addition, the further along the entrepreneur gets in reducing market, execution, and technical risk, the more likely he or she will be able to attract capital on better terms. Early actions should be directed toward reducing primary risks, as those risks determine valuation. The more one can prove market, technology, and managerial capabilities, the more the company is worth and the more likely it will be able to attract capital at reasonable terms. Thus, the achievement of key milestones, such as prototype development, customer acquisition, and supplier relationships, directly influences the level of perceived risk, company valuation, and the ability to attract investors. Furthermore, the entrepreneur should consider which milestones are most important to reducing the venture's risk and focus on achieving those milestones before other, less critical ones. In other words, it is important to ask what most needs to be done to convince investors that the venture is likely to succeed, and then to focus on those areas.

UNIQUE SOURCES OF FUNDING FOR THE SUSTAINABLE VENTURE

As mentioned earlier, sustainable ventures have some unique opportunities for financing that are unavailable to other ventures. Some of these unique sources stem from the fact that the benefits of sustainable ventures transcend financial returns and that investors are increasingly interested in financing companies that are aligned with their desires for a better world. But these sources also reflect growing excitement among investors for the idea that sustainable ventures will provide competitive, if not superior, financial returns. We describe six unique sources of funding for the sustainable venture, most of which have emerged relatively recently, yet are experiencing rapid growth and increasing opportunities for financing companies with positive social and environmental impact.

CLEANTECH VENTURE CAPITAL

Until about a decade ago, most high-level venture investors avoided clean and green companies. In the 1990s, renewable energy was out of style with the precipitous drop in oil prices in the 1980s, and most venture investors did not see significant financial gains in investing in green companies. That changed quickly with the advent of a new category of venture investing, *clean-tech venture capital,* which emerged soon after the turn of the millennium and followed an uptick in energy prices and concern with climate change. The concept, initially promoted by the Cleantech Venture Network (now the Cleantech Group), aimed to transform thinking about the economic potential of combining the venture investment model with technical solutions to emerging energy and resource challenges.

Clean tech does not describe a specific industry sector, but is more of an umbrella concept used to describe a diversity of products, services, technologies, and sectors that reduce environmental impact relative to alternatives. According to the Cleantech Group, clean technologies "provide superior performance at lower costs, while greatly reducing or eliminating negative ecological impact, at the same time as improving the productive and responsible use of natural resources."[2] The list of potential clean-tech sectors and technologies is large and perhaps surprising in its breadth, and includes renewable energy, energy efficiency, energy storage, agriculture, materials, recycling, and water treatment.[3] Table 7.1 shows the list of clean-tech sectors as reported by the Cleantech Group. Within these sectors, clean energy has probably received the most attention, and investments in solar, wind, biofuels, and energy storage have been prominent.

Clean-tech venture capital is mostly focused on profit-oriented, venture-grade investments. In other words, it is directed to companies with substantial economic and growth potential. It also generally refers to the activities of institutional and professional investors, who manage relatively large venture investment funds. What is most interesting is that global investment in clean-tech ventures soared in the last decade. From less than $1 billion in 2000, total investment in clean-tech start-ups increased to over $4.5 billion in 2008 and over $3.5 billion in 2010.[4] Moreover, the top venture capital firms in the world have raised substantial funds for clean tech and are aggressively investing in companies. Prominent venture capital firms like Kleiner, Perkins, Caufield, and Byers (KPCB) and Khosla Ventures have raised specific investment funds dedicated to clean or green tech investments.[5] Other venture capital companies, like Vantage Point Venture Partners or Braemar Energy Ventures, are dedicated solely to investments in energy, clean energy and/or clean-tech ventures more broadly. In addition, a number of large corporations with an interest in energy or other clean technologies are making substantive investments in clean tech companies. GE Energy Financial Services, for example, formed a joint venture with Conoco Phillips and NRG Energy to invest in innovative energy technology companies.[6]

Many clean-tech venture capitalists make it clear that they expect substantive returns to their investment activity.[7] Unlike some impact investors (discussed later) who are willing to sacrifice some level of profitability to achieve

TABLE 7.1 List of Cleantech Venture Sectors

Sector	Examples
Agriculture	Land Management, Natural Pesticides, Crop Yield, Sustainable Fertilizers, Precision Agriculture
Air and Environment	Emissions Control, Cleanup, Safety Monitoring/Compliance, Trading and Offsets, Clean Coal, Carbon/Emissions,
Biofuels	Biodiesel, Biomass, Grain Ethanol, Cellulosic Ethanol, Biogas
Materials	Bio, Nano, Biodegradable
Energy Efficiency	Monitoring, Buildings, Lighting, Building Automation, Heating and Air Conditioning, Appliances
Energy Storage	Advanced Batteries, Fuel Cells, Charging and Management, Other Energy Storage
Recycling and Waste	Recycling, Waste to Energy, Mixed Wastes, Waste Treatment
Smart Grid	Energy Infrastructure, Energy Transmission, Energy Management
Solar Energy	Systems, Cells, and Modules; Thin Films; Concentrated Solar
Transportation	Vehicles, Components, and Engines; Electrics and Hybrids; Fuels; Logistics
Water and Wastewater	Water Treatment, Wastewater Treatment, Purification, Filtration, Conservation
Wind Energy	Wind Turbines and Components, Wind Farms
Other	Renewable Energy Providers, Hydro Energy, Marine Energy, Geothermal Energy, Hydrogen Production, Combined Heat/Power

Source: Based on "Primary Sectors," Cleantech Venture Group http://research.cleantech.com/browse-taxonomy/, accessed July 18, 2012.

positive impact, clean-tech investors mostly pursue the traditional model of venture investing, wherein superior returns are the goal. Although some environmentalists dislike this approach, it signals the increasing alignment between the workings of the capitalistic system and better environmental outcomes. As we discussed in previous chapters, such alignment suggests that economic systems are changing to increasingly incent entrepreneurial actions that achieve sustainability.

All in all, the growth in clean-tech venture capital is nothing short of revolutionary. The magnitude of investments and the focus on solving critical environmental and energy challenges through technology represent a fundamental transition in thinking about the economic opportunities inherent in the transition to a more ecologically sustainable economy. For the sustainable entrepreneur with a high-potential technical solution to energy, water, waste, and other challenges, clean-tech venture capital represents a source of financing with unique potential to help start or scale their ventures.

IMPACT INVESTING

Impact investing refers to the funding of companies or other organizations with the potential to achieve positive social or environmental impact, beyond financial return.[8] The distinguishing characteristic of impact investments is that they are made with the intent of creating positive impact. Interest in impact investing is increasing rapidly, as is evident in the level of impact investments and number and breadth of impact investors. It is being increasingly argued that impact investments represent an emerging asset class because the processes of impact investments are unique.[9] Most important, impact investing implies the need for the evaluation and measurement of social and environmental impact in funded organizations.

Impact investors may target a specific industry sector (like health care or energy) or a specific problem (like disease or climate change) and fund businesses accordingly. Some investors are oriented to solving social problems, while others look to environmental challenges. Investment directed to solving social problems has become know as *social capital*, and the idea of social capital has generated a great deal of interest and excitement. Investments directed at enterprises in underdeveloped nations or impoverished areas are common and an important aspect of impact investing.

Impact investors' intention to create impact is typically in addition to the intention to create positive financial returns, although impact investors do not always expect competitive financial returns to their investments. In other words, they may be willing to sacrifice some level of financial return for the achievement of social or environmental returns. Financial returns that are below competitive levels are known as *concessionary returns*.[10] Impact investments made for longer terms than is normal have become known as *patient capital* or *slow capital* to suggest that investors are willing to wait for their financial payback. Thus, impact investments range from investments with primarily social or environmental objectives to those with primarily financial objectives with a secondary intention of creating positive impact. As such, impact investments may be made in nonprofit or for-profit companies. Impact investments also span a range of investment vehicles, including debt, equity, and program related investments into nonprofit organizations.

Impact investors also vary greatly, ranging from professional investment groups, to high net-worth individuals, to charitable foundations. Subsequently, we list some of the various types of impact investors available to the sustainable entrepreneur.[11, 12]

Social Investment Funds. A number of investment funds raise capital to invest specifically in social ventures. These funds may be comfortable with concessionary returns in order to invest in organizations with the potential for positive impact. Prominent examples include the Acumen Fund, responseAbility, and Root Capital. The Acumen Fund, founded in 2001 with the goal of encouraging entrepreneurial solutions to global poverty, was among the first organizations to embrace enterprise-based solutions to global challenges and eschew charitable donations in favor of debt and equity investments that have financial and social returns.[13] Root Capital is a U.S.-based nonprofit investment fund that invests in Africa and Latin America with the goal of maximizing social and environmental impact. It lends capital and expertise to small, rural businesses that might not otherwise have access to capital. As of 2012, it had lent $399 million through almost 1200 loans.[14]

Private Foundations. Foundations are increasingly interested in making program related investments and grants to impact enterprises. Some, like Ashoka and the Skoll Foundation, specifically direct their grants to social enterprises.

Impact Angels. Many high net-worth angel investors are interested in ventures with social or environmental impact. These angels target impact investments, particularly social ones. Although finding an angel investor can prove time consuming, a partnership with the right angel investor can prove fruitful, particularly in the early stages of a venture. In addition, the Investors' Circle and the Social Venture Network help connect social entrepreneurs and like-minded angel investors through events and other activities.

Social- and Sustainability-Minded Venture Capital Funds. Some venture capital firms have also shown a dedication to impact investing, or investments in areas related to sustainability. Although most of these are the clean-tech investors we discussed earlier, others focus on social businesses or specific sectors related to sustainability. Greenmont Capital Partners, for example, invests in consumer products ventures in the *Lifestyles of Health and Sustainability (LOHAS)* markets. With roots in the organic foods industry, Greenmont has invested in some exciting natural products companies like Izze Sparkling Juice, Blue Horizon Wild sustainable seafood, and Eco-Products (which markets compostable eating and drinking utensils).[15]

Banks and Corporations. Banks and corporations have also shown an interest in financing social and sustainable ventures. Banks may have access to federally backed capital for community development enterprises. Corporations like Google and Shell often create foundations that have provided funds to enterprises dedicated to solving global challenges.

SUSTAINABLE VENTURE BUSINESS PLAN COMPETITIONS AND PRIZES

As the trend of sustainable entrepreneurship has swept the globe, numerous universities, government entities, and other organizations have jumped on the bandwagon with venture competitions that offer prizes to the best social or environmental venture. Often, these are student competitions hosted by universities, but some are available to nonstudent enterprises as well. One of the first in the area of social entrepreneurship was the Global Social Venture Competition, sponsored by the University of California at Berkeley. Social venture competitions at many other Universities have also emerged, and prizes can be substantial. In addition, other universities are sponsoring clean or green business plan competitions, particularly in the area of clean technology. One of the first was the Cleantech New Venture Challenge, which started at the University of Colorado and now offers $100,000 in prize money.[16] Winners also earn a berth at the National Clean Energy Business Plan Competition, which is sponsored by the U.S. Department of Energy. In addition, business plan competitions of a more traditional nature often have special prizes for social and environmental ventures. Rice University's business plan competition, for example, has offered special prizes for both clean-tech and social ventures.[17] Finally, a number of corporations and other organizations have sponsored prizes for sustainable businesses and ideas. GE, for example, partnered with leading venture capital firms to establish the ecomagination challenge, which pledges financial and other support for innovative clean-energy technologies.[18] For both the student and nonstudent entrepreneur, these competitions offer a great way to garner seed capital for the sustainable venture.

CROWDFUNDING

Crowdfunding, an emerging and dynamic new means to fund projects and ventures, refers to sourcing capital for projects or ventures through a large number of small investors or donors, typically through a web-based portal. One of the most prominent is Kickstarter.com, which helps people with creative projects source funding to complete those projects. Project developers place their ideas on the Kickstarter website and request a certain amount of funding. Financial sponsors of the project pay through credit card and receive the satisfaction of being involved in exciting new ideas, as well as a small reward, which is typically in the form of the creative work that they sponsor. The crowdfunding model has grown rapidly, and Kickstarter sponsors have pledged over $350 million to 30,000 creative projects.[19] The crowdfunding model is increasingly being applied to venture funding, and the United States recently passed the Jumpstart Our Business Startups act, which enables the crowdfunding model to be used for equity investments in for-profit enterprises.[20] Many observers expect crowdfunding to grow rapidly and to support some exciting new ventures, particularly those with a social or environmental orientation.

Indeed, Kiva has been using a similar approach for years, allowing interested parties to make loans to help alleviate poverty. Kiva has already made over $300 million in loans through microfinance organizations throughout the world. They claim a 98.9 percent repayment rate on their loans.[21] However, as crowdfunding is a new and untested form of investment, both entrepreneurs and investors should be wary of emerging funding platforms because the risks of the models are not yet clear.

MICROFINANCE

Entrepreneurs who need loans for micro-enterprises may also access microfinance. Although no single, clear definition of *microfinance* is globally accepted, it is broadly known as the provision of small-scale financial services to people who lack access to traditional banking services.[22] Microfinance was first implemented for modern economic development in the 1970s by a small group of pioneering institutions. Among them were the Grameen Bank in Bangladesh, ACCION International in Latin America, and the Self Employed Women's Association Bank in India.[23] Each of these institutions thrives today and continues to make significant impact throughout the world. What's more, they have inspired numerous others to replicate their impact model and have demonstrated that people living in poverty can be a viable customer base for financial services. Yet, even with all the accomplishments that microfinance institutions have achieved, there still remain three primary challenges to providing financial services to people in poverty:

1. *Scale.* Growing the number of people that have access to micro-finance services

2. *Depth.* Penetrating areas that are remote and/or hard to reach, and reaching people in abject poverty

3. *Cost.* Decreasing the cost to micro-finance customers and service providers[24]

Even though challenges exist, there is potential for microfinance to play a powerful role in sustainable venturing. Grayghost Ventures, for example, is an impact-investing firm, with a $100 million microfinance portfolio. The firm has been a catalyst in growing the capital supply to microfinance institutions (MFIs).[25] More money than ever is flowing to areas of the world that have not had access to financial services.

Besides giving people access to financial services, microfinance has also been creatively used by sustainable ventures as a way to distribute products and create employment opportunities in economically depressed areas. VisionSpring, for example, is an innovative venture that took the concept of microfinance and has transformed it to create *microfranchise* opportunities for enterprising individuals in developing countries. Vision Spring's model is "to deliver high-quality, affordable eyeglasses to individuals in the developing world with a network of local entrepreneurs using a scalable model that reaches more people everyday."[26] They do this by loaning entrepreneurs a "Business in a Bag" microfranchise. The contents of the bag include all of the products and material necessary for marketing and selling eyeglasses, in addition to basic business tools like customer tracking and inventory management. VisionSpring entrepreneurs also receive training and support from local staff. The entrepreneur pays VisionSpring for the cost of the glasses once they have been sold. Using this creative model of microfinance and microfranchise, VisionSpring has been able to sell more than 610,000 pairs of eyeglasses and has generated more than $230 million in economic impact at the base of the pyramid.[27]

PHILANTHROPIC FUNDING

Nonprofit social or environmental ventures may also access donations from charitable organizations or individuals. In earlier chapters we briefly touched on the formation of a sustainable venture as a nonprofit entity, and although we have primarily focused on market-sustaining ventures, there is indeed a boom in the nonprofit sector that is contributing greatly to social and environmental causes. Since the middle of the 1950s, there has been astonishing growth in the number of nonprofits. It is estimated that the number had grown from approximately 500,000 in 1954 to over 1,563,000 in 2011.[28, 29] Although the competition for funding has increased dramatically, so has the number of dollars for which nonprofits are competing. Over the same period (1954 to 2011), philanthropic giving grew from $5.4 billion to $298 billion, in inflation-adjusted terms.[30, 31] Foundations remain the largest institutional giver, accounting for $46.9 billion in 2011, up 2.2 percent from 2010.[32] What's more, as the number of nonprofits has risen, so has the number of new foundations, meaning there are more potential funding partners a nonprofit can access. Although foundations are the largest institutional givers, individual donors are the primary capital source to the nonprofit world, accounting for $217 billion in 2011, about the same as in 2010.[33] The lion's share of the philanthropic funding goes to religious organizations (making up over 32 percent of all charitable contributions in 2011). The breakdown of philanthropic giving was as follows in 2004:

- Religious Organizations (32 percent)
- Education (13 percent)
- Human Services (12 percent)
- Health (8 percent)
- International Affairs (8 percent)
- Public Society Benefit (7 percent)
- Arts/Culture/Humanities (4 percent)
- Environment/Animals (3 percent)[34]

Although the legal entity of a nonprofit is indeed different than for-profit ventures, the crux of the investment or contribution decision for funders remains the same: It's about the value proposition. Funders of all kinds want to know that their money is being spent wisely and that their resources are being deployed in a way that makes the most difference. For all sustainable ventures, being able to track and measure impact is critical. This is no different for the nonprofit venture and is important for winning and maintaining donor contributions over the long term.

Summary

Obtaining financing to achieve the dream of sustainable venturing can be one of the most exciting moments in the life of a new venture. The prepared entrepreneur who understands personal goals, financing needs, and the advantages and disadvantages of various sources of capital is most likely to achieve funding that helps the venture succeed. The sustainable entrepreneur has a special opportunity to access capital from individuals and institutional investors dedicated to solving social and environmental challenges through enterprise. From clean-tech venture capitalists to impact angels to charitable foundations, entrepreneurs are partnering with funding sources that are aligned with their aspirations for a better world. Finding financing partners with similar goals may be a challenging process, but the ability to scale a new venture for maximum impact is one of the key rewards of sustainable venturing.

Key Learnings

1. Sources of funding for the sustainable venture vary greatly. Entrepreneurs can access friends and family, angel investors, venture capital, and a growing array of sources uniquely aligned with social and environmental ventures.
2. Financing for the sustainable venture may take the form of debt, equity, and even charitable donations.
3. Delaying the need for external capital through bootstrapping or cash flow generated from operations is often a preferable approach.
4. Setting a funding strategy for the sustainable venture starts with two basic questions: What are my goals for the venture? What are my funding needs?
5. When raising equity investment, entrepreneurs should understand the basic relationship between risk and valuation. Reducing risk prior to funding is central to increasing the attractiveness and value of a venture in the negotiation process with investors.
6. The four primary components of risk in a new venture include market risk, execution risk, technical risk, and financial risk.
7. Some of the unique sources of financing for the sustainable venture include clean-tech venture capital, impact investors, social and environmental business plan competitions, crowdfunding, microfinance, and philanthropic giving.
8. Clean-tech venture capitalists seek investments in a variety of sectors that reduce negative environmental impacts or enhance natural resources. They generally prioritize financial returns, even though they are investing in sectors that may achieve substantial positive environmental impacts.
9. Impact investors look for both financial and social or environmental returns. They may be willing to sacrifice some level of financial return for the achievement of impact.
10. Philanthropic giving is targeted to nonprofit entities. Like for-profit companies, funders want to see impact and a clear value proposition when contributing capital.

Endnotes

1. "Rebuilding HP's Garage," Hewlett-Packard, http://www8.hp.com/us/en/hp-information/about-hp/history/hp-garage/hp-garage.html, accessed January 16, 2013.
2. "What Is Cleantech?," Cleantech Group, http://www.cleantech.com/about-cleantech-group/what-is-cleantech/, accessed July 11, 2012.
3. "Primary Sectors," Cleantech Group, http://research.cleantech.com/browse-taxonomy/, accessed July 11, 2012.
4. M. Nordan, *The State of Cleantech Venture Capital 2011,* November 28, 2011, http://gigaom.com/2011/11/28/the-state-of-cleantech-venture-capital-part-1-the-money/l, accessed January 13, 2013.
5. "Betting on Green," *The Economist,* Technology Quarterly, March 12, 2011, pp. 22–23.
6. "Views from a Leading Corporate VC Investor," GE Capital, http://www.gecapital.com/en/insights-trends/insights/views-from-leading-corporate-vc-investor.html, accessed July 18, 2012.
7. "Betting on Green."
8. N. O'Donohoe, C. Leijonhufvud, and Y. Saltuk, *Impact Investments: An Emerging Asset Class,* J.P. Morgan, November 29, 2010.
9. Ibid.
10. Ibid.
11. D. Ransom, "Starting Up: Funding your Social Venture," *Wall Street Journal,* September 12, 2008, http://online.wsj.com/article/SB122124827514029295.html, accessed January 13, 2013.
12. O'Donohoe, Leijonhufvud, C., and Saltuk, *Impact Investments: An Emerging Asset Class.*
13. "About Us," Acumen Fund, http://www.acumenfund.org/about-us.html, accessed July 18, 2012.
14. "Our Approach," Root Capital, http://www.rootcapital.org/our-approach, accessed July 18, 2012.
15. "Focus," Greenmont Capital, http://www.greenmontcapital.com/focus.html, accessed July 18, 2012; and "Portfolios," http://www.greenmontcapital.com/portfolio-companies.html, accessed July 18, 2012.
16. "New Venture Challenge," CU CleanTeach, http://cucleantech.org/programs/nvc/, accessed July 20, 2012.
17. Rice Business Plan Competition, http://rbpc.rice.edu/About_RBPC/, accessed July 20, 2012.
18. Ecomagination, http://challenge.ecomagination.com/ct/b.bix?c=home, accessed July 20, 2012.
19. Kickstarter, http://www.kickstarter.com/, accessed January 16, 2013.
20. "Crowdfunding 101," National Crowdfunding Association," http://www.nlcfa.org/crowdfund-101.html, accessed July 20, 2012.
21. "About Us," Kiva, http://www.kiva.org/about, accessed July 20, 2012.
22. D. Karlan and N. Goldberg, "Impact Evaluation for Microfinance: Review of Methodological Issues," Poverty Reduction and Economic Management and The World Bank, 2007, available online at http://siteresources.worldbank.org/INTISPMA/Resources/383704-1146752240884/Doing_ie_series_07.pdf.
23. B. Helms, Brigit *Access for All: Building Inclusive Financial Systems* (Washington, D.C.: The World Bank, 2006).

24. Ibid.
25. GreyGhost Ventures, http://www.grayghostventures.com , accessed January 15, 2012.
26. "What We Do," http://www.visionspring.org/what-we-do/model.php, accessed January 16, 2013.
27. Ibid.
28. J. Wei-skillern, J. Austin, H. Leonard, and H. Stevenson, *Entrepreneurship in the Social Sector* (Thousand Oaks, CA: Sage, 2007).
29. Urban Institute, National Center for Charitable Statistics, http://nccs.urban.org, accessed August 1, 2012.
30. Wei-skillern, Austin, Leonard, and Stevenson, *Entrepreneurship in the Social Sector.*
31. Urban Institute, National Center for Charitable Statistics, http://nccs.urban.org, accessed August 1, 2012.
32. Ibid.
33. Ibid.
34. Ibid.

INDEX

sustainable venture, 4. *see* also financing of
sustainable venture
core values of, 84–86
elements of a successful, 82
legal structure of a, 95–97
measuring success and performance,
99–103
mission statement for a, 83
planning process for implementing,
86–95
venture team, 97–99

T

technical risk, 115
Terrapass, 9
Tesla Motors, 5
Thomas, Robert, 21
TimberTech, 71
Tom's Shoes, 54
Toyota Prius hybrid electric vehicle,
69–70
tragedy of the commons, 34
transactions costs, 41
Trees, Water & People (TWP), 56
Trex, 71

U

United Parcel Service, 6
United States Environmental Protection
Agency (EPA), 101
UN Millenium Development Goals
(MDG), 52
U.S. Organic Foods Production Act, 42

V

value proposition, 88
values of a sustainable venture, 84–86
Vantage Point Venture Partners, 117
venture capitalists, 110
VisionSpring, 122
voluntary industry initiatives, 40

W

Wal-Mart, 8, 58
watershed protection, 25
what if scenarios, 113
WhiteWave soy foods, 1
Williamson, Oliver, 26
win–lose scenarios, 19
win–win scenarios, 18–19, 60